Bessie Black and her husband Bob are retired missionaries. Beginning their married life as a farm couple in South Dakota, they moved into town, where Bob worked at a series of handyman-type jobs. Both felt the call to be missionaries (as described in her first book, *Once Upon An Island*), though wondered how, since as laymen they had no training for such. However, God needed them on several fields to relieve pastors from having to oversee maintenance at extensive missions facilities. Bob's experience was exactly what was needed. After seven years in two State-side missions assignments they served eighteen years in Papua New Guinea, Fiji Islands, and Solomon Islands as missionaries for the Church of the Nazarene. Bessie had many interesting and challenging tasks that proved it was indeed God who called them. They have now retired to Rogers, Arkansas.

Acknowledgements

This book could not have been written without the Church of the Nazarene and its great missions reach into all the world. It placed us in positions to serve in response to God's call upon our lives to be missionaries. In this our lives were enriched by knowing and writing some of these wonderful life stories of nationals. We particularly thank those in the South Pacific areas we served for nearly 20 years.

To our family and friends who kept saying, "Surely you are writing down some of these stories!" we say Thank You too.

My husband, Bob, has always been my champion, and best cheerleader. God himself knows how only He has brought me this far, by faith.

Finally, with my writing mentor and current editor, David Todd, it is now here in print. He took time from his own skillful and wide writing and publishing to guide and encourage me in this project.

ONCE AGAIN UPON AN ISLAND

Bessie Black

Copyright 2019

Once Upon An Island

Amazon Print Edition

Copyright April 2019 by Bessie Black. All rights reserved. No part of this book may be reproduced or transmitted in any form or by any means, electronic or mechanical, including photocopying or recording, or by any information storage and retrieval system, without the permission in writing from the copyright holder.

Front cover background from Google Earth,

Front cover photo by Michael Duncalfe; used with permission.

Cover designed by David Todd.

Once Again Upon An Island

1 "Tumbuna! Tumbuna! 1
   Papua New Guinea

2 Easter Week Trauma 5
   Papua New Guinea

3 First Fear..12
   From childhood to Papua New Guinea

4 Come, Now Is The Time To Worship, Scene 1 ..27
   Papua New Guinea

5 Is That A Real Missionary Job? 33
   Papua New Guinea

6 Heart and Hands—Do It! 41
   Papua New Guinea

7 Sit Down..52
   Papua New Guinea

8 Come, Now Is The Time To Worship, Scene 2 ..65
   Brisbane, Australia

9 The Mesmerizing Mongoose...............................71
   Fiji Islands

10 Fiji Island Friends...76
   Fiji Islands

11 Come, Now Is The Time To Worship, Scene 3 ..86
   Missions tour in Europe

12 Port Moresby: Painful Purpose 94
   Papua New Guinea

13 Just Enough 103
   Papua New Guinea

14 The Pharisee 113
   Olathe Kansas

Chapter 1

"Tumbuna! Tumbuna!"

"*Tumbuna, tumbuna, yu kam!*"—"Grandmother, Grandmother, come!", Little Margaret called out as she ran to me on the verandah of our little yellow bamboo home along the airstrip high in the remote mountains of Papua New Guinea.

Margaret's father, Mark, was the local pastor and had spoken to me of the trauma of another pastor and wife serving across the valley and over the next mountain. They had a brand new baby but the placenta had not delivered even after waiting for two days. In this remote place, in this situation… danger…death… was awaiting. Pastor Mark had received the shouted mountain-to-mountain message the day before. It related that men of the family would carry the new mother as far as our place. They would then seek others from this area to take her the seven or eight additional hours of mountainous trekking on to another grass airstrip where our Nazarene sub-health-center stood. There, trained nursing care was available.

I ran along with little Margaret to the end of the grass runway to find the group gathered. The men all stood, scattered wearily away from the burdened stretcher of burlap and poles lying on the ground. I rushed, weeping, to kneel and touch this precious young mother. She was so weak and fragile looking and totally unprotected from the sun. A young girl stood nearby holding the newborn.

"Bebe I bin pulim susu?" "Has the babe nursed?" I queried.

"Nogat." "No" the girl replied softly.

So I took the almost weightless life from her and put it to the mother's breast. This often effects the desired expulsion of the placenta. Still, sadly, to no avail. Through my tears I was overcome with anger as I comforted the mother and baby lying there in the dust.

I thought of what I had learned in our short time of being in this area. Though we had already served in Papua New Guinea for fifteen years and I thought I knew the culture, this newly assigned area had still more lessons for me. Here was great fear and challenge and responsibility for cause of death. In this particular case, it was greatly magnified. It was highly possible that while reaching the health center yet a long way off, she would die on the trail. To carry her as she died would surely make these men responsible for "causing" her death. Even attentively caring relatives would have to pay and would add not only to their personal grief but hurt their economy. No one in our area had answered the call to help either. Thus, these men, all of them, simply would not move on with this critically ill woman. Not even for one more dangerous mile. This shocked and hurt me so!

My grief mixed with anger towards these men and the culture, spilled out of my eyes and heart. Still holding the mother and baby, I saw Pastor Mark's bare feet nearby and heard his soft inquiry.

"*Besi, yu betin pinis?*" "Bessie, have you already prayed?"

Shame washed over me. Of course I hadn't, and I could only shake my head negatively. So he opened his voice to God in a simple request for help.

While his few words were still in the air, suddenly we heard above us the sound of a small airplane, circling. It was a total wonder. Planes came only on two regularly scheduled days of the week as long as we lived there, and this was not one of those days. Several of the now hopeful nationals ran up higher to the strip landing area waving arms and shouting at the miraculous pilot and plane, encouraging him to land. In only minutes he did just that.

Assessing the situation quickly, mother, baby, and pastor-husband were placed aboard. What would have taken seven or eight hours of back-breaking trekking now became only a five-minute flight. They flew over the dreaded trail and landed where wonderful nursing care waited.

Connecting via radio a short time later, I heard the great news, "We put in an IV and the mother responded and is doing fine. The baby is nursing, and all is well." Praise the Lord!

And so it happened. I will never get over my neglect and failure to bypass my own feelings and get on with God. But also, the joy of miracle in Pastor Mark's automatic assessment of the important over the urgent has stayed with me through the years. Also, I could not forget the fabulous pilots of MAF, Mission Aviation Fellowship, who sensitively cover the world with this ministry of caring for remote pastors and churches. When someone prays, and when a pilot is listening to God and just "circled over to look," miracles can and do happen.

Chapter 2

Easter Week Trauma

Tribal fighting was common in Papua New Guinea during our years there but had changed with the times. Now, instead of just spears and shields in daylight fighting, they had found access to guns. Trashy videos from overseas taught them about nighttime fighting and to how pose and shoot from the hip while wearing camo. They disregarded many of their historical fighting moors of honor and now rampant destruction and hate had become all too common. It pained us to see this with the lives of our dear nationals uprooted so painfully. Even with our years' experience, nothing prepared us for this Easter week tribal fighting that devastated a nearby Puri Village. A sense of foreboding flooded us as we took our Jeep, driving as far as we could go into that area.

This region was dear to us, especially the young adults who walked miles from there to attend the weekly Bible study held in our home. Often as many as twenty came. We were blessed as they sang with their guitars and flutes and we learned together. Once there was a police action in the area and curfew was set. They had to be back in their homes when it was dark, by 6:00. Because of this difficulty, I asked them if they thought it best to cancel for a time.

"Nogat tru!" they said. "Of course not! We will just come two hours early." And they did.

Another time it rained torrents and since rain, to them, is dangerous and full of evil spirit activity such as lightning and storm, they usually are not out in it. Yet here they were this night at our door, dripping wet. How glad we were for a fireplace and my mug collection, which I had wondered if I should even bring along to PNG. I served them hot chocolate as they slowly dried off by the fire. We had a crowded, damp living room but full of blessing.

Now had come the Lenten season and Palm Sunday. We heard of fresh fighting there in Puri, and wanted to see if anyone stayed and if the church there was still standing and to worship with them if so. We frequently left the Kudjip Nazarene Hospital campus to wind our way to bush churches to keep in touch with nationals. Now here we were, stepping out of the Jeep, looking around in disturbed awe at the devastation. It was eerily quiet. Not a sound—no bird calls, no rustle of leaves, no workmen sounds, and no church music in the air welcomed our arrival. The whole area in front of us and as far as we could see was destroyed. We parked right where an educated man had built a wood-framed home. He had put in glass windows and a verandah and had enjoyed his community along the road. There in ashes it now lay, burned to the ground.

The whole area had been shades of green with tall banana trees, and Yar trees among the valuable coffee trees, planted in tight rows throughout that whole area. Now, as far as the horizon, our eyes saw open space with fresh greens all over the ground. Every coffee tree was cut down, the long years of labor planning and caring for this valuable cash crop wiped out. Hate-filled hands wielding machetes and axes had done their work. Gone were the tall Yar trees, that give shade to the coffee trees and add nutrition to the soil, now of no use. Long banana leaves lay strewn all around in thick, painful display. These had been badly needed for food and also for bride price exchanges. This sea of green shot a brilliant dagger to our hearts.

We whispered as we walked slowly, our feet cushioned along this green swath, down and across to a large single-log bridge towards what we hoped would be the still standing church. The government had made it a law to never burn a church in tribal fighting but many rules went by the wayside when fighters' 'blood was up'. We were speechless as we moved across the quiet carpet of fresh green. All of a sudden we heard a faint strum of guitar and hope filled our hearts. As we got closer we saw the small frame church still standing and rejoiced. A few very old women were swaying outside, weeping deeply. They beat their breasts and waved their arms up and down in grief. The young Bible College graduate pastor met us outside in quiet sadness. He shared how they had at least not burned the church. The fighters had taken the nice linoleum they had placed across the platform and had taken other items. Soon inside, we noted that the wooden pole pews remained and the few people, mostly old women, were weeping quietly and listening to the hesitant strum of Joe's guitar. His head hung low as he sat on the front row, but I was comforted to see him. Joe worked for me at the Nazarene Book Store. He was a fine Christian, an able and educated young man. He and the pastor were the only young men—the only men at all—who had stayed. It could be dangerous for them but they had risked it for this service. For this Palm Sunday moment. We sat, just praying aloud along with them, hearing their mournful weeping.

Soon I sensed the pastor come close to me and ask, "Bessie, do you have anything for us?"

What a question! What could I have for them? What could I do? What healing was there? As farmers in our early years, we knew the loss of all that agriculture, and the loss of the years already past to get it to the place of profit they had the day before. Now all was lost. *How could I help?* Yet, we had learned as missionaries that we always, always, did have something for them. We had news of Jesus Christ. We had the Good News. So I responded with a quiet

"Yes," and he led me to the front of that small sad group.

Seeing their tear-filled eyes lifted expectantly, I felt God's peace and began to share. I spoke of the devastation we had just walked through, fully known to them of course, and our feelings of pain for them. I shared of their loss, the terrible and irreplaceable loss. I recounted the downed greenery, the lost economy, the lush bird song now all gone, and the new home now only ashes. They all nodded in agreement. Then I felt the Lord lifting me to share this actual Palm Sunday day. As we had walked across that hacked green blanket, I had thought of that Palm Sunday of long ago when Christ rode the borrowed colt along another green path into Jerusalem, with shouts of joy, waving branches, and acclaim.

How short lived that was! In just a few days it too was all gone and He, our Christ Jesus, hung dead on the cross for our sins. How sad. The end. The finish. The emptiness. The devastation. His friends scattered, all alone, no one to help. He had died. He was placed in the tomb, wrapped as usual for the dead, and the tomb was well sealed. Time passed as the disciples wept and mourned, as the women wept and mourned, as the world around them wondered. Time, lots of time, passed. He was really dead.

Then came Easter Sunday! Then it all changed. Then He arose! He left the tomb empty. He appeared unto many. This evidence was astounding. It was physical, it was emotional and it was real. He did what he promised to do. He changed all that devastation into joy! Into possibilities! Into new hearts. Into what he wanted it to be. It was not just about Him as a great rabbi or a prophet but about Him being the Son of God, our victorious Savior. When He ascended back into heaven, He sent them the Holy Spirit to live in each of them and work out his wonders. All over the world the painful loss, and the devastation in our human lives, would now become seed for what God wanted originally to do.

So today we too felt this with them. This devastation leading to new seeding, to newness in our lives. Not pain free. No, but weeping with purpose and promise. If we let God work in us we will see that this Palm Sunday, of green devastation, and the crucifixion in the next few days, turn into Easter Resurrection Sunday with the redemption not only for each of us but for our whole world. We prayed for each other. We sang praises. We lifted each other, and we each went home to celebrate Easter which was already coming to these hearts.

Out of this group of Puri Village young adults, still coming faithfully to our home Bible study, came a manager for the Nazarene Book Store; in time a pastor and his wife; then too, a talented artist to draw the colorful, pictorial Bible teaching charts so useful in this still somewhat illiterate culture. The guitarist of that day later invited us to his wedding and rejoiced in what

God had given to him. The old women were able to weep again but with joy, and as time—lots of time—passed, God moved and new life sprang up once again where formerly only devastation wounded eye and ground. He Lives! Still!

Chapter 3

First Fear

When I thought about it, it seemed that I lived a charmed life. As a young girl I joyfully lived everything. I was excited about everything around me and adventure was in my DNA. Being number seven of eight children probably helped, and being the youngest girl brought its own rewards.

I loved the Wisconsin farm where I was born and where my father had a cow, a horse and chickens. I was interested in them all. Hanging around close to the soft cow while Dad milked her, anticipating my cup of warm milk, was a treat. When Dad sprayed the cats in the face, they too loved the sweet lickings. One day the rooster must have felt invaded by my three-year-old eagerness and he rushed at me, pecking sharply in my forehead. I saw the fear in my Dad as he readied that bird for supper right then. *"He could have taken your eye out!"* Still, I was not afraid. I sorrowed when our horse old Dick died, and I saw the men in my family dig the grave out in the pasture. But fear was not a part of that sweet farm life for me. Though still so young, it was probably born in me then that I would always want to marry a farmer.

As I grew, we moved to the city, Superior, Wisconsin, where Dad worked in the shipyards building Liberty ships for the war. I became the first in my family to attend kindergarten and loved it so. Those rhythm instruments! The snacks of milk and graham crackers! The sunny patch on the floor where I ran with my little nap rug to claim a spot! All was just so wonderful to me. Adventure daily! For the long winter they flooded the school grounds next door to our home, thus creating a wonderfully huge ice rink. Skaters filled it with ice shows of skill. I wore my big brother's skates, which made my feet and ankles bend inappropriately. With the painful, crashing results, I still never lost my love for that icy experience. At that early age, I walked to the dairy store a few blocks away, even in winter, for our big jug of milk. With Mother's home-made woolen mittens and snowsuit, what was there to not enjoy? What was there to fear?

Next we were on to Cedar Rapids, Iowa. Here were new places for this nine-year-old to behold in the city center and huge residential areas to explore. We kids walked the entire city whenever and wherever we wanted to. We trooped with friends through the downtown area. With my siblings, I fearlessly crossed the railroad bridge over the Cedar River and on to

Sunday school. In the winter we tasted those frozen steel railings with our tongues. I loved a dare. In the summer I went with my brothers to the city dump where they shot rats with their bb guns. We took potatoes and roasted them in the hot fires of rubbish burning all around. The dump was a wonder to me with all that fun stuff! Adventure! No fear!

As a pre-teen I loved the many friends I met in school and the neighborhood. We enjoyed exploring. We walked miles to get to the free zoo and see the bear. We met the circus as it unloaded down at the train yards and followed along beside the swaying elephants through the brick streets. On and on, up to the grassy fields, where they erected huge tents where they would perform. It didn't bother me to have to walk back the miles home either. Such interesting things to fearlessly do.

I loved to sit with a friend at the cemetery, in the stone gazebo, or just walk about looking at the monuments and flowers. I was never afraid of the dead there. Across the street, the large, three story high school offered wonderful places to climb into or jump down from. In winter, when snow drifts were deep, I climbed even higher to land in that soft heap down below in the window wells. During those years, daring was such a part of my joyful life. The activity of jump rope called to me. Faster and faster! More and more! Though my Dad feared it would hurt my heart it was never too much to my thinking. The game of jacks with friends was exciting too with its competition. Our scratched stone markings on the sidewalk gave the game some boundaries. Of course, these were not for me, just for others! I loved the game's challenges.

I loved being on the edge of excitement and fear. Unfortunately, it meant I tested right and wrong too and often did not choose well. Stealing candy bars from the corner drug store was simply a fearless challenge to me. Taking money from my Mother's purse was a fun event. I was a happy-go-lucky sinner those days, all the while knowing Jesus as my Friend. Thankfully, my conscience was pricked one time in church and I knew I had to repent and confess to the drugstore manager. I needed to stop this sinning. Without any adult knowing or supporting me, I took my money to pay him and headed to the drug store. I can still see him talking to me as a young girl there. He wore a dark suit. He put his hands behind his back and bent over a bit to listen to my confession and repentance.

He then asked me, "Why are you doing this?"

My response was, "Because I want to go to heaven."

This changed my definition of sinning. I was no longer thrilled to steal and grew in grace in those years. In my Christian home, and with a great Sunday school and church, my heart bloomed. Excitement and challenge still held me fearlessly but with a new bent to my heart.

In the evenings, I loved to help my Dad with his second job, wallpaper hanging. We went to homes and I pasted while he measured, cut and hung the lovely new wallcoverings. We climbed ladders and fearlessly moved back and forth on scaffoldings. Of course, huge Hershey bars were tucked in the equipment grip for me. So all was well. I was learning and I enjoyed this adventurous time.

Dad knew we needed a second bathroom and, though he was not a plumber, accomplished this. I loved to watch and hover over him as he worked. He showed me how he was just learning to do the very dangerous part of molten-leading of the pipes to connect and seal them tightly. He wore a huge, heavy, canvas-leather-like glove on one hand. In this he melted the solid lead, using a blowtorch. He then rolled the joined pipes in this liquid to cover and seal the joint. Dangerous work and new for him, yet I felt his fearlessness in myself and was awed at this production.

I used to fearlessly take myself to the dentist. With painful tooth and with a bill clutched in my hand, I walked the several blocks toward the dentist's office in the city center. It was along this route that I observed the tall spire and stained-glass window of the Catholic Church. It attracted my exploring heart and wondering spirit. My little Protestant Nazarene Church was plain and simple with its short stucco bell tower. With this edifice so tall above me, it called me to peek inside. Of course, I was not afraid and never gave it a thought as I opened the heavy door and slipped inside. In those days, churches were always open. When my eyes adjusted to the dimness of the sacred interior, I checked out the holy-water fount, the pamphlets, and the poor box. The sound of the shaken coins was probably what brought the priest to my side, and thus we met. Totally fearless, only very interested, I spoke. He could well see he had a curious young Protestant here and asked me if I would like to see the Stations of the Cross. Of course I would! I will never forget his kindness and interesting way of sharing these wondrous pictorial carvings along the walls of the sanctuary. So interesting! The Bible stories I already knew now came alive in front of me. I felt I was "right there with Jesus" during those days so long ago. That sense of holy awe stayed with me as did my high regard for the Catholic Church and this priest.

    My Dad loved to attend many churches and upon occasion enjoyed the African American one not far from us. When he asked who of us kids might go along with him, I always said an eager yes. Now in my junior high years, my school had a diverse ethnic mix, Bohemians, Syrians, and African Americans. And we all seemed to get along well and be involved in the same things. Thus, I looked forward to this adventure. I loved new things and seeing new people and places just fit into my desires. We walked to the sweet church and enjoyed the service. I loved the opening and its worshipful pageantry as the white-gloved and robed choir came swaying down the aisle with their joyful music. The preaching with audience responses was so interesting. I loved it and was never afraid in this differentness. Other times Dad took me to the street corner services the Salvation Army band held downtown. I loved their trumpets and drums and uniforms. Never mind the bad weather, snow, or rain. I was always eager to go.

In all this living fearlessly as a teen, and loving every minute of an exciting, adventurous life, danger lurked in my heart. I had not seen how Satan was trying to cause me sinful pain. I had come to Christ as a young nine-year-old and loved spiritual growth in Sunday school and Bible reading and memorizing Scripture. I eagerly attended church. Yet my spirit of adventure still took me to the edge of right and wrong many times. I tested and tried things that could cause me pain and regret but did not fully see it at the time. This was just an adventure for me. What new thing could I try or get into. Fear? What fear?

In eighth grade I met a crisis. I had always loved school and gotten good grades easily. I really liked my teachers and readily did my school work. Still, there was this one, with the odd name of Miss Cop. I felt it would just be such fun to tease and make some trouble for her. It would be fun for me anyway! I convinced some of my friends to go along with me. We watched the clock and when it struck the hour, we would all just immediately jump up and shout out a cheer. What fun it would be to startle her and disrupt the class. Sure enough, at the appointed hour we all stood up and cheered and disrupted the class along with our teacher, Miss Cop. I was successful! It was such fearless fun!

Later, walking down the high school halls basking in my latest bold classroom achievement, I sensed another teacher who I greatly admired following me, seemingly with intent. She always looked so nice, wearing a suit and pumps. She was so good at her teaching and loved us students. As one of her straight-A students, I felt it especially. I just knew she wanted to talk to me and suddenly I was worried and chagrined with this imminent encounter on my heels. I thought to myself, *"I will just slip into the girls' restroom and surely will lose her. She won't ever want to come in there!"* Was I ever wrong! She followed me right inside and there spoke softly to me. Now, as I look back, it felt as if we were all alone in there, but perhaps it was not so. Still, it is frozen in my heart and mind as she talked with me.

"Bessie," she said, looking kindly into my face, "what is this I am hearing about you in other classes? It doesn't sound like the wonderful girl I know. I'm surprised and hurt by this news."

As she went on to kindly chide me with her loving words, my heart was broken. Repentance filled me right there and then. It washed over me as I saw myself for what I was and it shamed me in her sight. I don't remember more of that conversation but I do remember how it changed me. From then on, my exciting adventurous ways did not involve causing pain to others, nor involving my friends in dubious behavior. It seemed that the Scripture I had once memorized had done its work. "The fear of the Lord is the beginning of wisdom." The respect and awe of God that I had been taught now held me. I sensed new wisdom as I saw that not only was I displeasing a favorite teacher along with Miss Cop, but I was displeasing to my Lord and God. Now, the right kind of fear was invading my heart and behavior.

A life of adventure still followed me as I turned fifteen and moved with my family to South Dakota. I realized my longtime dream of marrying a farmer. He was sitting right there in church and besides that had a new car! Too exciting! As a young bride my farm life was daily a joy and interesting challenge. I learned to control my city girl ignorance of animals. I could actually gather eggs while wearing leather mitts. I could raise a baby lamb and chase sheep out of my garden! I loved to take coffee out to the field for my man when he was plowing or harvesting. We often walked through the tree stand on our property gathering stumps and branches to burn in the heating stove. When our horse broke through the ice on the pond, I ran to get Bob's dad and a rope and soon all was ok again. To me, it always seemed that there was a way to go or something one could do when encountering danger or a problem. So, actual fear did not have an opportunity to enter into my great farm years.

God began to move in our lives, taking me and my family from the farm, into town, and on to other places. He was calling us to be missionaries. Fear did not have a place in these decisions for me. It was just a huge call to adventure and excitement in God's will for us and His good care. The cultural changes only added to my love for adventure and challenge and excitement. Always meeting the new. Always seeing the new. Always tasting the new and different fed my life long spirit of open eyes and heart and hands and feet. God was giving me the adventure and excitement I had always been drawn to. I was a blessed woman in all of this.

At our first assignment, as stateside missionaries, our time with the Native Americans took us to the reservation homes of nationals. We ate wonderful, awesome foods together, and worked with kids for hours in camp meetings there. It seemed each day brought a "new thing." Spiritual warfare was all around that culture but it never brought fear to my heart. I felt cared for by my God and blessed in this gift from Him.

We loved our next assignment with students in the Latin world. With their coming from Mexico and so many Central American countries, different for sure. Interesting and exciting too. As I began to learn Spanish l was led into an expansion of interest that was amazing to me. My eager, adventure loving heart just unfolded into this people. The privilege of joining in with them in so many cultural activities certainly fed my desire for the different and wondrous. Here too, I knew many had deep cultural fears but I felt none of this personally and was often able to be of help. I am grateful.

When we were next asked to serve in the South Pacific, in the young but developing country of Papua New Guinea, we quickly responded with an eager, "Yes! But where is it?" It's easy, in a way, to do so when you don't know much about where you are going nor what you will be facing. *What new things? What new kinds of people? What changes will be necessary?* The wonder of the tropics pulled me. We heard about the perfect weather too. The prolific gardens producing year-round in abundance spoke to us. Living where there were palm trees? Having our own avocado tree for our beloved Mexican food? Wow! A new language to learn? Never mind, *maski,* never mind, it would all be great. An adventure for me. Saying 'Yes" to God came easily for me. A joy and another exciting look into a new world and people group. Leaving our now young adult sons, we departed the USA eagerly along with our two youngest, now teens.

Flying to this southern hemisphere island just north of Australia, took hours and hours. We were exhausted when we arrived at the small highland airport in this new country. The crowded, dusty, room serving as a terminal was daunting. We were met with the cheerful kindness of new co-missionaries. They helped us with getting our luggage and family settled into the van and onto the forty-five-minute trip to the Kudjip Nazarene Hospital, where we would be working. Being where almost everyone was black was startling. Just looking out the windows as we rode brought us to the newness of it all. Dense greenery was interspersed with coffee gardens along the way. People, lots of people, walked along both sides of the ragged blacktop highway. Adding pigs to this pedestrian group made it even more colorful. All seemed unconcerned about their safety. Still, we had a good driver and I drank it all in.

Nearing our destination, we suddenly saw the road ahead of us covered with shouting men. They were warriors we were told. Ready for war, they had blackened their already dark skin with ashes from fires, and wore only narrow loincloths. Their long, dark, glossy cassowary feather headdresses vibrated upon their heads. Their hands held shaking, long, bamboo spears with carved arrow heads on the sharp ends. The tumult was all around us in the van. Our driver slowed. He seemed just casual as he could be as he rolled down the window and chatted with these excited fighters. It was reported that the local two tribes were warring, a common event, and they were awaiting the enemy there. We learned that only the fighting tribes were involved, no others, nor were we ourselves in any danger. Our driver soon cheerfully left the men with words in their own language and we rolled on slowly through the group and into the hospital compound.

After a short stop to unload our luggage, we were introduced to the whole missionary family in a homey, social gathering. With good food and loving words of welcome we knew we were here now! As it grew late, we soon eagerly went to retire in our new temporary home. We tried to settle in. We were finally here and all alone on this darkening first day. Though my travel-weary family was soon in slumber, I was wide awake and tossing and turning. In my mind's eye I saw the blackened faces of warriors at each and every window. In my imagination, I kept hearing those angry shouts I had heard out on the road. Their glistening, black-feather headdresses shook at me. I felt the darkness closing in and felt my first great and mighty fear. It shocked me! It swallowed me! It held me captive! It startled me and I was powerless against it. I could not sleep. This very new and total fear was paralyzing me. It was the very first time I had ever felt this way. My first fear. And terrible in its grip.

As I dealt with this all alone that first night, I worked it all out. I decided that this hospital compound was large. It was fenced. It was where I would be working. And I could do just that and never need to leave this safe place for the roads, where danger lurked. I could stay inside the fence and do what I was asked to do. I would be busy and careful and somehow live with this great paralysis within.

Morning finally came and with it my new resolve, held within myself and unshared. There was so much to be doing and arranging for with our family and new home. It kept me busy. Very busy. I explored the compound and hospital. I learned about the work of Bob and myself and the schooling plans for our two high school kiddos. We plunged into the language and cultural learning. Being busy was a big help. It swallowed the fear—or at least shrouded it.

I don't remember just how long this lasted. A few days, a few weeks, perhaps a couple of months Its duration is lost to me. But one day, I do so well remember, I was sharing the depth of this fear with a dear new co-missionary friend, the same one who had picked us up at the airport that fateful day. She too remembered the scene we had driven through.

In hearing my heart's cry, she said, "Bessie, I don't think God has brought you here to give you a spirit of fear. This is not of God. He has given you a spirit of power and of love and of a sound mind."

All of a sudden, I heard this wonderful Scripture for what it was. It was true. I had memorized it long ago as a child and knew it so well. Now, I claimed it for myself. This fear was not from God. He has given me power, and love and a sound mind. Not fear. Just recognizing these words from the Bible made my soul's window open wide and God's refreshing, cleansing, healing air rushed right in. My fear was instantly gone! I was filled with peace and the deep fearful paralysis was gone.

That First Fear was the last. I do not remember a single time in those next eighteen years in mission involvement in PNG that I was ever afraid. We had many times of danger, and unknowns, and wonderings, along with health changes and loneliness away from our family, but never fear!

On top of all this, while obeying God's call upon my life as a missionary, He continued to give me craving for adventure, love for the new experiences, new cultural excitement, new foods, new language, and love for brand new souls saved, and even more. I had daily new events all around me. Often it came in nationals' village homes, or as we welcomed these new friends into our own, out on the dirt roads to bush churches, or hiking through the coffee and tea plantations. The area markets were always so interesting. We never tired of these ways of God in letting us enjoy what He had called us to do and be here in this wonderful country. We just seemed to be living a precious life.

Now, in our retirement years this pattern has continued. No fear. Just great adventure. And all with a great God who knows the path I need to take. "He has not given me a spirit of fear. But of power and of love and of a sound mind. "Thank You, Lord."

Chapter 4

Come, Now Is The Time To Worship

Scene 1

On our very first Sunday in Papua New Guinea, our teen daughter, Laurie, and I decided that we were not going to "let ourselves go" in this primitive place, and so prepared for worship that day. We put on our nylons and Sunday dress shoes and went with our family to church. It was a beautiful cross-steepled building at the edge of the campus of the Kudjip Nazarene Hospital in the lovely South Pacific tropical highlands. It had been constructed as a memorial to Sydney Knox, the first missionary in PNG for the Church of the Nazarene. The air was fresh from the last evening's rain and the sun was bright. Nature certainly set a blessed mood for expected worship. As we set out for the short walk, we found no sidewalks—only the very lightly graveled road and wet grass to cross. In minutes our nice shoes were wet and getting muddy. Our hose and edge of long skirts also held the remnants of the heavy nighttime rain.

As we sat on the plank benches among the women on the female side of the church, we noted the feet of those around us. Most were barefoot. A few wore flip flops, or slippers, as they called the sole-only, rubber ones so common there. I saw the occasional tennis shoes, perhaps worn by hospital staff. Not a nylon to be seen. We were the only ones with Western dress shoes and the only ones with still wet and muddy feet! We soon figured out that the bare footed ones had only to wipe the mud off outside on the abundant grass to get clean and enter. Those with simple shoes likewise. Our plans to "not let ourselves go" were "let go" right then and there.

All this distracted my worship, of course. Without understanding the language, I sat there chilled and quiet. Though a few of the songs were in English and we could join in, the beat and strum of the guitar did not match. All the newness distracted my intended worship that day. Still, we met new friends and shared what we could in greetings as we streamed out at the end of the service.

We adjusted to our assignments and work but soon knew that for us, we must get away from our work site, the hospital campus, to really know the nationals where they lived. This meant going out on Sundays to those "bush churches" which we had heard about. We looked forward to this intriguing experience and the next Sunday our language instructor took us to a nearby village area. The church there was built of flattened bamboo woven walls and topped with long *kunai* grass bundles to keep the rain out. This was typical of the bush churches.

We were greeted warmly though without understanding, and soon entered for the service along with the cheerful villagers. The room was lighted only by the open door and windows without glass or screening. The floor was dirt. The seating was narrow, split trees placed over very short stumps. This made seating really a form of squatting. So unladylike! I was glad I had by now learned what to wear and had on a full skirt. And I was now, wisely, in my tennis shoes. I so longed for what I had known as worship. I missed this and needed it so. As we settled in near the back, our instructor whispered cultural encouragement from time to time.

"See that man near the front with the white t-shirt on and with only leaves at his backside for trousers? He is a church leader here and a wonderful Christian."

There was a lot of skin exposed throughout the church but I tried to ignore it. Seated there, I felt culture shock after culture shock rush over me. Our feet rested on the dirt floor as did everyone's. At least it was dry. The singing was in the local language and hard to listen to. It sort of had a strident tone with odd starts and stops. Without any warning, I was next startled by the young child in front of me. When she turned sidewise, I caught an awful smell. Pus was running out from her inner ear and down her neck! I was shocked, and could not help staring. When she saw my eyes were on her, she turned again to the front. I felt so sorry for her and was disturbed.

    The cackling of a hen running along the narrow central aisle caught my attention next. Soon it was hurriedly and noisily chased out. From somewhere else there was the peeping of a chick. Turning, I noted it to be within a *billum,* carried by a woman sitting close to me. This wonderful, woven-string bag was good for lots of things. Our instructor explained that the young chick was safe only here in her bag. Left at home, it might have been eaten by some creature or perhaps even stolen. Thus, the valuable chick must come along to church.

    I tried to follow the sermon as our instructor had shown me where the scripture was in the Melanesian Pidgin language New Testament. I looked at the line drawings in that version and tried to think of what was being said. I noted on that page a drawing of the disciples in the boat with Jesus and tried to imagine what the national pastor was saying. Later I found out that was not the sermon at all, the picture had simply been on the same page. So many languages are spoken here that an interpreter was needed for the pastor's sermon to help those who were from other distant language areas. I learned that they were probably workers from nearby tea plantations. As a young mother interpreted for the pastor there on the low platform, her small toddler decided he needed her attention too. Soon he crawled from his seat to the dirt floor in front and climbed the short rise to her on the platform. Without missing a word, she cuddled him to her bared breast and while he was being satisfied, she kept on translating. No one noted this except me. I was shocked! Finally, the last straw for me seemed to be the mangy, village dog running around among us. Loud shouts sent him back out, but his interest in the service was greater than mine and he kept returning.

With cramping legs, sore bones, and frustrated with what I was experiencing, I cried out to God within myself, "God, this is not worship! This is not being in church with you! This is not Scripture! It is neither where I want to be nor where I can sense you. Where are you?"

As is the pattern with Him, He so lovingly responded. "Bessie, worship is between you and me. It is just between the two of us. It is for you but for me too. It is not the trappings; it is not the building materials, nor the look of the people, certainly not the languages. I know them all! I know your language too, so I can understand what you say to me and what you desire, even if you don't say it out loud. You can worship me right here in this place. You must, perhaps do it only within at first, not outwardly. Perhaps quietly or even with your eyes closed at times. You must shut out what distracts you because it is getting in your way. Not so for these other worshippers here. They have discovered how to worship me. They know how. Now you must learn this too. Worship is between you and me. Your heart will learn to connect this way here in Papua New Guinea. In this strange and different place, we will enjoy each other's company once you get this down pat. Be blessed. I am here waiting for you always."

I did settle. I did close myself in with the Lord. I did finally worship that morning in that new place. God met me there and I met Him.

I had one more great startling moment at the end of that service. The church leader, who had been sitting on the front row with his back to me, the one pointed out to me earlier wearing the white t-shirt and only leaves for trousers, came up to shake my hand and greet me. With that experience I really did have to concentrate on my cheerful greeting as I read the flowing words on the front of his thrift store t- shirt, all in blue glitter: "DISCO FEVER"!

Chapter 5

Is That A Real Missionary Job?

There was a time, when to me, a missionary was sort of like a picture I had seen of one wearing a pith helmet, carrying a huge Bible in one hand and wielding a machete in the other, trekking through the African jungle with a lion on the trail ahead of him. His goal was simply to get to people no matter the danger and share Christ with them and save souls. This pictured scene did not let me think of much else in this role and calling. Thus, some years ago, when I heard of someone appointed as a Nazarene missionary to start a bookstore in South America I was startled.

"How was that a real missionary job?" I asked myself. *"Where was the lion in all of this? How was that sort of very ordinary job saving souls?"* This question was not totally answered until many years later, in my own call and work as a missionary.

Along the way, God had given me new light, as He often does with us. I found that even my own "normal", my own "ordinary" sort of skills had been used by Him in our stateside mission assignments. Before ppointment as a Nazarene missionary, I had been a Montessori preschool teacher and found my skills useful on the campuses where we were asked to serve. In both of our two stateside appointments, I developed a small Montessori preschool and taught the preschool children of students in our Native American Nazarene Bible College and later in our Spanish-American Nazarene Seminary. This provided parents a safe place for their children to learn while the parents were in class, preparing for the ministry. As an added benefit that the parents could see, Christian education for these little ones started them well and early for school later on.

Sharing with these families became a rich ministry for me and opened my eyes to the mission call other than the "lion on the trail" picture. I soon saw that there were many "lions" outside of Africa. The need for spiritual bravery was strong in the role I was fulfilling. We loved to have student families in our home and hear their national life stories and legends, while sharing food and fellowship. Thus I was in a position to strengthen spiritual growth in these families and offer encouragement. So often it was badly needed when they were far from their reservation home or were from another country, and student life seemed hard. It was personally fulfilling to sense that God had found a way to use me—to use just what I could do—to use me as a missionary for the big mission picture.

During our nearly twenty-year assignment in Papua New Guinea which followed, I did a variety of work. I was asked to start in the finance office of the Kudjip Nazarene Hospital doing work I had never done before. As is usual with God, He made this possible and productive with His help. Added to this, I particularly enjoyed leading Bible study and conversational English classes in our home. I was asked to teach a class in the college of Nursing and also in the nearby Bible College. That was new and interesting. Across the valley, at the wonderful Catholic girls' agricultural school, I was invited to teach evangelism for a group. In high school-age boarding schools in our area I found a rich blessing holding weekly student Bible studies. Many of these young people went on to become pastors, nurses, teachers and good Christian family people. Even now with the Internet, we have heard from many of them and their current ministries in a variety of circumstances. All this surely made me see that the many ways of God to reach the souls of the world are not always just what I had thought, but fill the need of the day and times in these many different cultures.

A small supply room on our hospital campus was a place where pastors could come and buy Bibles for their use and for sale in their villages as needed. For years it had met the need, but now that need had grown rapidly. Our own church publications department in PNG was constantly printing new literature for pastoral as well as lay use. As many more people became literate, things to read were in high demand. The Bible Society printed Bibles and other booklets, including some in recently translated languages of our area tribes, which were becoming available.

My hospital finance work was now being done mostly by skilled nationals and the need was being met. Thus, when asked if I was interested in taking on the small Bible sales spot and perhaps developing it, I was really pleased. By this time, I well knew that, even though I had absolutely no experience in business, God could train me and it could be accomplished. I accepted this new role with faith.

I looked over the mostly unused former school building at the corner of our hospital campus grounds and saw possibilities. Though a small building, it had two large rooms, a smaller one, and even an indoor toilet! It was near the three hundred student community school started by our early missionaries and across from the large Knox Memorial Church. All this was alongside a very active road from the village above the hospital down to the road junction where several small stores and a huge fresh market did business daily. A well-trafficked connection for small buses was there also. I could see this central corner as a good place for our Nazarene Book Store to begin to bloom.

With the aid of our hospital carpenter we installed counters and shelving. The Coke distribution center gave us a small refrigerated glass case for sodas. We added boxed juice and milk drinks, along with pretty apples. With so many school children coming in from the community school, we wanted to sell some healthy snacks—along with the local crackers so beloved. One room was designated for the art work of making the well-used charts for teaching illiterate villagers. Bible stories for Sunday school lessons and for other topics were drawn here. Designed with symbols and colorful markers, this had already proved to be a wonderful way to teach. Sunday school teachers could simply hang this large poster-chart up on a tree outside, or peg them into the bamboo walls of the church, and an attractive lesson was ready. Young men could draw these in this room. It would be an easy place to secure at night and all would be ready for them the next work day.

Now I needed to find national employees for the new store. We sought Christians who would be trusted with materials and money. I would be there daily but needed others to help. Planning ahead for future national management was also important. In our weekly Village Bible Study group in our home, God showed me a great young man who proved to be just right for this managerial job. He was also a sign writer, having graduated from art school after completing his high school years. He painted a great sign for the new bookstore and installed it on the corner of our lot so all who came and went, by the thousands, would see it and perhaps stop in. He was faithful and responsible with money also. So, now we had staff.

To start, we filled the store with Bibles, always sold at cost with no markup at all. Now to find ways to sell other products needed by the area and to make money to pay our staff and maintain the store. The local elementary school students had been going to faraway stores for their school pencils and notebooks, supporting non-Christian businesses. As we soon were able to supply these school needs, we saw it as a blessing. The children could now walk this short distance, never crossing a road, to get supplies at a reasonable price and also support the mission work. All profits would go to our PNG Nazarene Publications division to continue printing needed literature.

Pastors, with difficulty, had been ordering guitars from stores twelve hours away on the coast. Now we supplied this much-desired church musical instrument. Our College of Nursing students loved coming to get Christian cassettes, Christian t-shirts, and good reading in both the common language and English, which they had used throughout their education years. But most of all, the hospital was our market for literature. Even sick people loved to read. They seemed to crave it. I often saw nationals walking along the roads reading a tract or lesson. Any tract or bit of literature was happily accepted, never refused.

Our hospital saw thousands of health needs monthly and both patients and their visiting families enjoyed the presence of our store. Many would buy something to take to their sick family member. The Nazarene Bookstore was soon a successful business and ministry arm for our publications division.

The many markets around the area were open daily with crowds milling around. After shopping for the wonderful fruit and vegetables grown in local gardens and available year round, the people loved to spend time gathering with friends. We could see this too as a wonderful outlet for our ministry of Christian literature. But we needed sellers. Soon we found seven young men who would take a banana box full of items and go by bus to these outbound markets. They would lay a small piece of plastic out on the dirt and place these words of God upon it and share Christ with this literature. In addition to Bibles and small New Testaments, pens and pencils, notebooks, and some other small booklets and tracts were made available. We heard many accounts of God using these to change lives. Naturally, we soon saw our profits increase, and after paying our staff we could see our publications division ministry being blessed financially. The printing presses were busy.

As I worked with these young men daily, I saw them grow in grace and responsibility. It blessed me to see the work they so enjoyed for the Lord. Our start to the workday was with devotions. These young men could really pray! My life was enriched knowing them.

This Nazarene Bookstore was just the place for me those years. I love to meet people, love to chat, and love to help. God blessed my days in this work. So many would come in to browse after visiting a sick family member. I could see that they were often discouraged, frightened or even crying. It was my joy to share Christ and prayer with them. I could suggest some small item of literature that would lift their spirit. Or, if they had no money, I had some wonderful free items to share. Some of these had been sent from home churches, such as unused Sunday school papers. Some had been for children and were colorfully attractive, fitting the need so well.

So many people! So many waiting! So many ways to reach them! So many willing to help!

Hmmm! What is a real missionary job? What is in your own hand?

Chapter 6

Heart and Hands—Do It!

I was gathering our mail at the little post office shack. It was used by the missionary staff in Papua New Guinea at the Kudjip Nazarene Hospital for personal mailing and delivery. It also had a fun Swap Box, a library, a place for sharing extra pineapple from our own lush gardens, or just for reading posted notices. The mail was regularly picked up at the PO in Mt. Hagen, some miles away, and brought here and sorted by one of us missionaries. Large boxes of used clothing or medical supplies sent by churches or friends frequently had to be unload. This was just the site that fit it all. As I finished my gathering and stepped out, there he was, a trim teen Papua New Guinean boy who seemed to be waiting for me. And so I met Layapi. I loved to meet new ones here and so quickly engaged him in conversation.

"Yu stap orait yia?" I asked. "Are you okay?"

"Mi orait, tasol mi gat liklik wari." "I am ok, but have a problem," he responded.

A common greeting and a common need in PNG. Yet this what we came for. To come for the multitude of "problems" and to help them find the answers that Jesus gives to fit them all.

As we talked outside our campus post office, Layapi shared his story. He had come from a distance and been hired to work in the compound maintenance department but had just had a terrible experience. At work one day the assignment was to clean out the septic pit at the College of Nursing girls dorm. The men set to it wearing rubber boots and using long-handled shovels. It was hard and messy work. But the very worst was that as a young PNG man he was placing himself in great personal danger just standing in this feminine product. His culture had warned him that he could "lose his power, his manhood," in just such a situation. He must avoid it at all costs. Actually, any excretions from anyone's body were to be avoided at all times.

It so upset him that he ran in fear. He took a small bus and rode the long way back to his village. There he felt safe. There his national pastor met him. Upon hearing his sad story the first thing this good man asked was, "Layapi, have you been paying your tithe?" It was so direct and so moving for this young man to hear. He replied, "No, I have not been faithful in this." Even though he had become a Christian believer and had *"tanim bel"*, or turned his stomach (which, unlike the "heart", is the seat of PNG emotions), he still had spiritual growing to do. The response was so kindly given to him, "Pay your tithe, and go back and go to work. Humble yourself, son, and do it." Though startling, Layapi accepted this for the wisdom it was and here he was back at Kudjip and back in maintenance employment. Now, he was looking for some way to advance.

I could easily see the quality in this young man and wondered if he might be the answer to my own prayers. My work at that time was in the financial and accounting division of the hospital. I was responsible for the payroll for the station workers, the nursing staff, and the student stipend. Also, I attended to the front office answering the hospital phones. Just recently we had need of a new man to do that particular phone work. *"Might Layapi fit in there"?*

Typically, time here was not important and so we had plenty of it while standing there. He shared his life story and I fit in my questions as to his ability for this work. He told how he had no sisters so had raised his own pigs. This job was usually women's work, but he had been able to pay for his schooling himself. Since there was no free education, he took on this hard work as a young man. He had finally finished the common elementary grades of 1-6, all done in English, and had done well. The two of us went from speaking the common national Melanesian Pidgin English and on to English to see how well he could handle this part of the needed phone work. He was surprisingly clear. He was about fifteen years old with only six grades of school. Since it cost a lot to attend high school and since one must test well to be selected, it was highly probable he had gone as far as he could in education. This was the all too common scene. I grew excited as he spoke and I could see the possibilities. He certainly was above the level needed to be a maintenance worker. I suggested he apply for this office job and as we both would pray, let's see what would happen.

Shortly, as I had hoped, the job was his and we began a journey together that blessed him, the mission and the hospital, and me. In times not needed on the phone, he became skilled in helping with the payroll cash and accounting. He was adept at seeing error. He could so well make the bookkeeping corrections and became valuable in all the financial paperwork needed. In time, we noted that for him to continue in this level of employment, he needed the proper "paper", as they say here. He needed more than his grade six degree. Happily, he was eager to take the high school studies by extension offered by the government and paid for his own first course. We were glad to help with even more studies. He sold more of his own valuable pigs to continue in this. He arranged on his own for the use of the evening study hall, joining the College of Nursing students there. This gave him the needed time and quiet place after his regular work day to accomplish this good thing.

His pursuit of education was a joy to see. When in time he completed the four-year courses needed to graduate from high school, we all rejoiced with him. Here, as in the British system at the time, grade ten is the finish of high school. These helpful years from Layapi blessed the hospital's medical work so. From phone work, his new direction was more fully on to the finance division.

Soon added to his regular work was the new financial saving plan by the government. This was for all hospital and mission campus employees. Similar to our Social Security, some was paid in by each employee and the government added to it. Setting up this new program needed a good man with a good mind and Layapi was a fit for this skilled work. He proved to be trustworthy and honest in accomplishing this.

At this time, one of my own missionary assignments was the weekly shopping for the hospital. Taking the van, I drove the miles into Mt. Hagen and spent the entire day with this work. I first banked money, a nerve wracking time. It entailed standing in a long line with many trying to squeeze in ahead of me. Then on to pick up nails, paint, lumber, tires, and a multitude of other items for the maintenance department. Next head to the medical supply center for oxygen tank refills or other hospital needs. Often I picked up cases of bleach that had been ordered. Perhaps fabric for dorm curtains was needed. The mess hall for students might need items not available from the hospital's extensive gardens. Shopping for my second favorite work place, the Nazarene Christian Book Store on campus, required many different stops for the needed inventory. Add picking up the mail at the town's PO. All this—all those boxes—had to be crowded into the van. Lastly, getting formal paperwork for departments at so many offices with their odd hours of work, took time and patience.

Taking Layapi with me on these weekly trips proved to be so valuable. In addition to being my security, he took care of all the money and banking business. He knew where and how to acquire the ordered items and was thrifty and insightful. His blooming skills were so needed as our hospital grew and government requests increased. I was always glad he came along on shopping days.

These were years when Layapi was thinking about a wife. He wanted a Christian wife and was careful in this. In PNG it is the girl who can be aggressive. It is culturally possible to be married by just eating a plate of food given to you by an eager young woman. Gifts, too, were a part of the bride price and receiving them might be an agreement in advance. He experienced this. One day I noticed he was wearing a nice pair of slacks. Though he had always looked professional in the office these were definitely brand new. When he told me that they were a gift from a man on behalf of his daughter, I was concerned for him. It would have been hard to say no to this fine gift but he and I both knew there were strings attached. This was from a non-Christian family. As he shared his own concerns we prayed together about it and he soon returned the gift. It seemed good to him that he did not get entangled in a marriage out of his faith. He wrote a long serious letter to me in thanks for my help and support in this decision.

As I could see Layapi's value to the hospital work, I also felt some loss for him. Since we were by now really good friends, one day I felt I needed to talk to him about a subject dear to me.

"Layapi," I started, "it is wonderful that you can do all you do for us here. You are trusted to do the banking, and business and so many decisions with quality and honesty, but here you are letting a white woman," (to use their way of speaking), "drive you around! Why?"

His answer shocked me as he admitted that he could not drive. He had never been taught. He had never had a chance to learn.

That set my mind in motion. I told him how I had taught my mother to drive when she was over fifty years of age and I could teach him too. I would ask Bob if it was ok and we would use our little yellow Suzuki jeep and it would get done. He could pay me $2 each lesson for benzene (gas, which was $4 a gal at that time) and that would be all. We could practice in the area school grounds after hours and on quiet dirt roads nearby. I could see how happy this made him. Here he was, a godly, mature man with a business mind and ability and still with this huge need. Seeing this as a good solution, he agreed.

Of course, Bob was more than happy for this to happen, so Layapi and I set off for him to learn this enhancing skill. He took me into the ditch only once and even then we just went right on up and out. Whew! He was jerky and stiff with this new thing but careful and patient. In time, he was doing the driving for me as we went on the highway into town. This gave him more good practice and at greater speed. Even so, it was only about 50 mph.

After quite some time he really wanted to take the driver's license test. I felt a bit reluctant but decided to go ahead for his sake and try. On to town, all excited, we went. He had not driven much within the small town but with its slow pace I hoped it just might work out well. I waited while the officer took him on this momentous journey. When they returned, I could see Layapi all smiles and happily getting out of the training car.

The officer however, sternly approached me first saying, "*Missus*, I think you must give him a few more lessons."

I felt badly for Layapi who was approaching us now all lit up with joy! Then he asked the officer if he passed, and in typical PNG style, telling one what they want and expect to hear, he responded with a "Yes, you passed." And it was done. Just like that. I had taught Layapi to drive. With his smiling face and new license in hand, we headed for home.

After that we had only one traumatic driving day. It was when we were coming home from Mt. Hagen with our little Suzuki full of supplies and with Layapi driving as usual. By now, he had gained skills and ease and I felt secure with him. We reached a narrow, one-lane bridge about half way home. We were going slowly as usual, when up from the tall kunai grass alongside the road raised a bunch of *rascals*, criminals. Of course, they were intent on robbing us or stealing the jeep. They leaped up onto the hood waving machetes, shouting in chorus to stop us. Without thinking, I told Layapi to put it into third gear and keep going slowly. He quickly did just that and we progressed, losing the *rascals* in our wake.

But they had a Plan B, didn't they? Across the bridge, fellow *rascals* were waiting in the long grass and now suddenly threw up onto the road a long differential from some old car wreck. Instantly it was just there in front of us with its iron shape strong and slanting across to block our way. Somehow inspired, I told Layapi to keep it in third gear, head for the lowest end and bounce over it, and keep going strongly. He did that and, with a strong hit and bounce, we were past the danger and shakily on our way. It all happened so fast that I never felt afraid nor had time to do anything but just what we did. Layapi did amazingly and, as we got back home, we both were grateful for our stout vehicle. We also knew angels had watched over us on that bridge.

After all this success, and with him now carefully driving other vehicles solo too, I was happy for him. One day he called to say he wanted to speak to Bob and me together at our home and so we gladly invited him over. He stood formally in our living room, in front of Bob and with serious face, thanked Bob for allowing me to teach him to drive. He then held out a $100 bill for Bob as payment! Wanting to reject this, of course, we both reminded him that we had agreed on only the $2 each lesson for benzene and no more. He had long ago paid that. We shared that I was glad to do this for him and it was our pleasure to see him succeed. But then he spoke of that time when the *rascals* tried to stop us on the bridge and how dangerous that was and what could have happened. He said "No, Bob, I must give this to you because I could have killed your wife!" We now could see with his PNG cultural eyes that very truth. For if I had been hurt, he as the driver, would have been held responsible. We could see that he was still painfully carrying this guilt. So Bob graciously accepted the cash and Layapi breathed a sigh of relief.

In the following years we have seen this good man married to one of our nurse aids from the hospital. He became even more valuable in the business of health ministries through our church and with the national government. Our mission has been blessed with his many abilities and his work ethic. His children know their father is a good and honest man. He now also has businesses of his own, expanding his work both in our area and back in his home village. Other mission opportunities have opened for him.

As for myself, I saw that I was blessed to see biblical principles carried out in me, for in that what my eyes saw to do, I did. And with all my heart I put my hands to the needed work which, at that time, just happened to be on a steering wheel. Yes, just a steering wheel. How blessed I was!

Chapter 7

Sit Down

In Papua New Guinea, the Kudjip Nazarene Hospital campus is large and spread out. It is bordered by the Waghi River along the East, a village and mountains rising to the South, the highway and community market area on the North, and tea and coffee plantations spreading to the West and, really, almost all around the campus. With Bob's assignment as co-maintenance missionary to maintain the hospital and the area around it, he spent a lot of time at first just walking to and from jobs. Soon he and others saw that he needed to be places quicker than his feet could carry him. He gratefully accepted a Honda motor bike. Now he could be way up the campus to check our hydro dam, then down to the national homes where staff and nurses lived. He could quickly head to the community school and teacher's housing, and even to the pasture and gardens where food for both patients and College of Nursing students' meals were grown. The endless maintenance situations within the walls of the hospital itself took a lot of attention and shared knowledge between him and his many workmen. Having the bike now worked well for these multiple needs.

Bob got used to it and flew up and down our dirt and gravel campus roads supervising in those areas. The hydro particularly required frequent attention in those days, as did worker instruction. The men needed continued training as many were still learning how to weld, lay concrete block, build coffins, put up wire fencing, do lawnmower repair, and so many other hospital maintenance requirements. Though Bob had never managed men as foreman, or *boskrew,* he quickly found out that they usually only needed his quiet direction or presence. He did his best to fit into that need.

While two of my evenings were spent having students and community nationals in for conversational English classes, Bob began to love going up to the village, often carrying a pineapple from our garden. He sought out meeting the men, sitting around their fires, talking, telling stories and listening to them. He found ways to share Jesus with them, help them bring family members into the hospital, and often pray for them right there. These were all new ways for Bob. Since he only used his bike for campus work, he grew to love the walking. In those early years he went up those trails barefoot. It was only later he needed shoes, as glass bottles had come to PNG and often lay broken on the roads. He loved to trek longer distances to meet the people on the coffee plantations, sometimes heading out early in the mornings to catch them before they had gone to work. He did this many Saturdays, learning much and aggressively making friends all over.

After sending him out, most of my Saturdays were spent at home greeting the many knocks at the door. Wonderful nationals came with gifts of produce, questions to ask, and social calls by the many loved ones we had grown to know. By now we were both able to share their language and converse and pray with them. Bob now loved the hugely crowded community market place he would have normally shunned. Here were sold the many wonderful vegetables which grew year-round, the hot steamed sweet corn still in the husks, and wonderful tropical fruit so inexpensively purchased. The bits of lamb meat browned on a sheet of metal over a fire always made his mouth water, *spet i pundaun*. This was his regular ten cent treat. Here people gathered to talk, sell, buy, and occasionally fight. Tribal differences blew up here, multi wives caused friction that became visible here and old slights over pigs or land ownership could flare up so easily. Small stores abounded around the area. He particularly loved to meet the aged tribal fight leader, now these many years a Christian. He loved his hugs and talking to him, and Bob always had a bit of money to put into his hand. These outings away from hospital campus work gave Bob balance. His love for this country and his calling from God became very real and practical to him. Those he met became special to both of us and we often had them in our home. Some came for meals, some for overnight sleep in front of our fireplace, some to share their legends and histories with us over a cup of Milo, and others with a need of counsel and prayer. God led us both into these new and unexpected ways of being a missionary. Our first three years in PNG sped by, fulfilling us both.

Suddenly, one day, this all came to an abrupt halt. As cars and trucks carried patients into the hospital grounds, they came up a short, flower-lined road to the immediate emergency area. This made for quick connects with the nursing staff and the rapid assistance needed. On this day Bob was riding his bike there, and as he came to this road, another vehicle crossed in front of hm. He had no time to divert and they crashed. Bob's bike and head hit the side of the incoming van and he fell loudly, bike and body and all to the ground. Here in the midst of patients with their family members siting on the grass awaiting care, and in this very busy place, a rush of the crowd to his side was immediate. One national told me they had never seen "a white man turn blue like that!" Bob was unconscious. He was quickly carried into the hospital's single private room we had at that time. As Bob lay there coming around, his color returned. Dr. Evelyn Ramsey, our surgeon, quickly assessed the situation. She was a talented doctor and ably checked him out.

No broken bones. No blood. Only a few sutures were needed on his lip and she took care of those. I was at home. Called by anxious voices, I just then arrived at his bedside. I was so glad for the speedy care right there at our own hospital and felt God's hands as they worked over my man. His bed was surrounded by national nurses and friends all crying and praying and showing great concern for Bob. They knew he had stepped out of his own comfort zone and taken the time to know and to love them.

Bob had never gone out onto the highways with his bike nor sped down the dirt and gravel roads outside of the campus, so he had not seen the need for a helmet. Now, with this injury looking minimal as to head wounds, we breathed a sigh of relief and felt gratitude to God. After his healing came to his lip and his dented cheekbone, he seemed to get better and soon was back to his old self, working carefully and feeling good again.

It was not long though before I began to see changes in Bob. He was back at his usual work and bike riding and worker management, but now was showing some physical difficulty. He felt unsteady. He was always tired, weary, "a bit off", as the Aussies would say. In checking with the doctors at the hospital, they thought he might have a mild case of malaria. This disease, along with pneumonia, is one of the two main killers in this country. Of course, we had been taking the usual treatment to prevent this. To give him a rest and a bit of a break from the work, it was decided to send him to the coast with another missionary family, just to let him rest and drink up the great ocean breeze and sand. I needed to stay at our assignment so he "took his medicine" and went reluctantly alone. He enjoyed walking over the black coral beaches and seeing the ocean. He rested and devoured the sweet coastal mangoes there in that area. He felt better and so did I when he arrived back home after a couple of weeks. He was grateful for his co-missionary having filled in for him and now took up his share of the load again. If it had been malaria, it would soon pass and he would again be on his bike rounds with the men, pulling his weight.

Sadly, Bob continued to be very subdued. I thought he was adjusting until one morning he admitted to me that he had a hard time even putting on his jeans. He could not balance well. It startled him and me too, of course! I talked to one of our doctors, so busy with the rush of patients, and shared this new happening. I asked a nursing friend what she would do. "I would get my husband to a hospital in Australia as quickly as I could," she replied. These words woke me up. Bob was in serious medical trouble and it was unknown just what and where it was. Quickly our doctors saw to it that he was sent to the larger Mt. Hagen government hospital an hour away. Here he could receive tests unavailable at our own hospital at that time. The Indian doctor there took her small tool with a metal spiked wheel and ran it over places on Bob's body. It told her he had something in his head that had caused these problems but just where this was she could not identify. They did not have a CAT scan at that time or many other skills or equipment. All these were common problems for this third world country.

Because of this, the decision was made for Bob to be immediately transferred to Brisbane, Australia. It was the hospital closest to us with the ability to assess his medical needs. Friends packed my bag for me, someone gave me a small purse with Australian money in it, and flight tickets were arranged quickly. One painful last thing was to talk on the phone with our three adult children in the states and our Paul in school five hours away. It was painful to let them know of this trauma and our plans. Now even more than distance would separate us. The great unknown with their dad's health loomed over the phone calls and would linger with them after the goodbyes. We were blessed to know that our teenaged Paul was in our Nazarene Hostel at the wonderful high school on the Wycliffe Bible translators center campus and cared for by loving hostel parents.

All needed arrangements were made for us by loving mission staff, and the long flight proceeded across the South Pacific. As we flew, Bob and I held hands and he told me he thought he could just die any moment. We talked of this. We felt God's peace as we calmly agreed that it would be ok even if this happened. Our lives were given in happy obedience to God. Our children loved Him too and those back in the states were mature believers. We felt blessed. We arrived in Brisbane and spent a sleepless night in a hotel while a hurricane blew outside the windows.

In the morning we were taken to the wonderful Royal Scottish Presbyterian Hospital. Interestingly, their wonderfully awaited CAT scan apparatus was not working, so we spent another day wondering, waiting until it could be fixed. When the scans came back it was very apparent that Bob's head injury had been much more serious and damaging than previously thought. Given our limited equipment in PNG, it had not been visible until now. The wonder of a CAT scan! It showed how Bob's bike accident injury to his head, seemingly thought to be mild, had set off slow bleeding just under his skull and against his brain and now had pooled. This subdural hematoma was now putting pressure there, causing his current problems, and would certainly cause more if untreated. The doctor told me that even on the flight here he could have just coughed and had a stroke or died. It was so close!

They took him immediately to surgery. With burr holes put in the right places, the pooled blood was drained. It would take more surgery and a second set of burr holes placed for additional drainage. Eventually, a trephine, which cut a circular bone out of his skull, finally cleared it and released all the pressure.

The doctors now felt operations were done and it was time for him to heal. We settled in to do this. Bob's stay in the hospital was long as continual infection became the enemy. Still he kept positive and we both were hopeful. The mother of one of our missionaries had kindly offered me a place to stay. I took the train to the city from her home early each day, and back again in the evening. Daily I stayed with Bob to see how it all went.

After three months of this hospital care and treatment, the low infection was still a problem. One day I received word that, when dismissed from the hospital, the mission had decided that we were not to return to the PNG field yet. The roads there and on the mission station campus were rough and it was felt that Bob would not do well recovering under those conditions. Also, with the still present infection, they decided that he needed continuing US medical care.

It was startling to know that the usual four-year term, for us, was now to end at just three. What would happen to us? How would Bob recover? Where would we live and get treatment? And finally our hearts' cry would be felt with this request: "Would our return to Papua New Guinea ever be possible?"

All these questions were in my mind as I headed to the hospital that day to share this disturbing new plan with Bob. Of course, we had talked of how good it would be to soon be well and able to again return to our beloved PNG and what we would do there. Bob had continually talked of his national connections and his workers and village friends. He longed to see them again and just be there in this land he had so grown to love. Seeing Paul again would also be wonderful. But now I had to let him know the change of plans and I knew his grief would be great.

I spent the day as usual with Bob, reluctant to open this wound yet. He loved to have me "Read some Abraham to me," so we often read and reread Genesis and were encouraged. It was the fragrantly productive grape season there and I had walked to a small fruit stand to bring this multicolored fruit to share during the day as the hospital did not have a dining room for the public. The doctors' visits were regular, and I had the opportunity to ask questions. We believed we had such good care. He would find out that the doctors had approved his leaving for the US if he had an appointment with a neurosurgeon there right away. This was being miraculously arranged in California. Finding all this out would make Bob feel better I was sure. The day was passing when I realized I still had to talk about this with him.

Finally, I told him the mission's decision and medical plan and the reasons for it all. He heard of the directions from his doctors as to his health needs. I shared how our pastor back home had called to tell us they already had an apartment ready for us. They wanted Bob to share in a service right away even if all he could do was stand and greet everyone They loved him and wanted to see him, their visible answer to prayer.

    I tried to be positive, but Bob's sadness was palpable. He could not grasp that he was not to be able to go back to PNG and say "goodbye" to everyone. It was just not done! To leave so suddenly would be too sad. He would not be able to go to the market or up to the village, or on to the plantations and shake hands and let them know his thanks and see their faces once again. The past three years sort of slipped away and he felt bereft. How could he just leave this way? We both wept and prayed and hugged and in time I had to leave to get the train back.

    Alone now, Bob lay there on the bed feeling lost, empty and abandoned by me, the mission, and even his own body. He mourned and cried. He felt all alone. He had certainly questioned me and now He questioned God. Finally, as was his usual bedtime activity, he reached into his bedside drawer and pulled out his Bible. He loved to read it and had often found answers to meet the needs of the day. This time it just sort of fell open to the gospel account where Jesus fed five thousand people the miraculous banquet of bread and fish and how they all got their fill. A wonderful event with many blessings hidden in it. This time though it was at the start of the story that God opened his eyes to a new thought.

When he read, "And Jesus had the people sit down," he felt as if it was said to him personally! "Bob, sit down." It was as if Jesus was saying, "I have placed you right now in a place in your life where I want to do a big miracle and feed you a feast. You don't even know about it yet. You can't see it yet. You didn't feel it coming! But listen! First you must 'sit down.' Just like the crowd to whom I gave the bread and fish banquet, they had to first get ready for it and 'sit down.' Now you too need to submit to me." Bob yielded as he lay there. He felt God's peace. He felt God's direction. He accepted and believed and rested in Jesus right there in that hospital bed.

Later as we flew home to the States, I wondered, as Bob had too, if this was our "goodbye" to the South Pacific. Would we ever return to our beloved PNG and missionary work and blessings there? Over the ocean God gave me a message from Psalms 107 to cheer me. There the sailors were out in stormy seas and crying out, wondering if they would ever again see their desired haven, their home port. My personal prayer for us became these sailors' same cry. "Take us back safely to our home port, our desired haven!" For us this would be our beloved PNG.

I felt God saying to me, "Yes, I will either take you back to your desired haven, your beloved PNG, or I will change your desire. And it will be good either way."

This promise rested us as we flew home. We found wonderful total healing in God's hands with US medical care. Bob immediately started to recover as the infection was soon totally cleared. We were able to do our whole year of home assignment services as well and, within thirteen months, Bob and I were once again back on beloved PNG soil. We did return to our "desired haven". We feasted on God's miraculous banquet those next fifteen years in PNG mission ministry. Bob was so often made to be glad that he had submitted to God's direction, just as He had directed at the feeding of the five thousand: "Sit down."

Chapter 8

COME, NOW IS THE TIME TO WORSHIP

SCENE 2

It was nearly three years into our missionary assignment in Papua New Guinea, when the motorcycle accident disrupted our missionary lives, and we were forced to go to Brisbane, Australia, for surgery and care. Thus, Bob and I found ourselves in a new place, a new country, new trauma, and without family or friends. Our hurried travel plans had been kindly made for us and with good hospital and surgical care here, we now prayed for speedy healing for Bob. We soon found it was not to be simple. The subdural hematoma was a serious brain injury and careful skills were needed in order to heal. God had given us these careful skills in ample supply and with multiple surgeries to come, Bob would be progressing well.

During these days, I stayed in the home of the mother of a co-missionary from the PNG field. She was kind and caring. I started my days taking the city train from her suburban home to the hospital. At the end of the day I traveled the reverse to her caring food and sleep. With no car, nor desire to leave Bob alone, I did not get out to church. As the weeks stretched out, I longed for the blessing of communal worship. One special day I was invited to attend church and worship with a Nazarene family there. They also asked me to lunch in their home afterward. This meal part of the invitation was especially tempting, as the hospital did not have a cafeteria for the public, nor were there any restaurants in the area. I had cold sandwiches sold at the hospital gift shop or leftovers from Bob's tray for my daytime meals. Of course, I never intended to accept the invite but in talking with Bob, he had another idea. He said, "You go. Then you will have something new and different and interesting to tell me all about. I need to hear about this too. So you go. I will be happy for you and I am not alone here with such good care."

With his encouragement, I accepted the invitation and made plans. Real Sunday worship and a real Sunday dinner! After years in PNG with no need for "Sunday clothes", I would need to buy an outfit for church. It was exciting to do this in anticipation of the wonderful worship service I would be attending soon. I found out that they would be serving communion that day and that it was a church with an organ. It all made a longed-for picture in my mind and it grew large in my great anticipation. Real worship! A real church! Real pews! Real worship music! Yes, I had loved the PNG worship as I had grown to participate and feel God's presence and his wonderful ways of working in my heart in new ways of language, and cultural aspects. But now, thinking of what awaited me in a first world country, I was in a total state of excitement and worship anticipation. I so needed this! True, I had meditative visits to the hospital chapel, and I read the Bible daily for long hours to Bob. He often said, "Read Abraham to me again!" So, I did. But now, faced with this approaching Sunday in my own former cultural worship ways I built the event up to heights of joy and wonder. I could hardly wait for the appointed Sunday to arrive.

Arrive, it did. These wonderful new friends picked me up and we were off to church. My heart swelled with joy and spiritual longing. God would meet with me this day in a new and blessed way, I knew.

Seated in a real church pew I looked around at the stained-glass windows with awe. It was startling to see the color and designs. As the organ rose and the hymns sung, I was conscious of the volume of the sound and even the holding of the hymn book as we stood. It was all new to me once again. Later, seated, I found myself staring distractedly about. Now I saw others in dresses. Others in heels and hose! The new pastel hose at that! I noted others with their hair all freshly done up, and many with makeup. It was so distracting for me. I could not take my eyes off them. There was a special singer that day, but it was almost foreign to me because I startled to see that he had a microphone. And that he walked across the platform slowly, back and forth as he sang. I never got the words as my ears did not get a chance to work with my eyes doing all that discovering. I know they had communion that day, but it was totally lost to me. I probably was too interested in the fact that they used real communion wafers…not broken hard crackers, and had real communion cups which we did not have to share. Plus, they all had such clean hands! The only active thing of mine that morning was my eyes. They were roaming all around the church! My heart was far from worship that day.

My plans, my intentions for meeting with God, my own idea of what worship would be, my personal longings and knowledge of worship would be shocked this day. It would shake me and make me over. It would teach me, and once again I would be renewed in ways I did not anticipate. Not then. Not at that moment. But in time to come, I saw what God had taught me about worship that first Sunday in the village church back in PNG. Now this Sunday in Australia, he would re-teach me what He desired in worship from me. What it was all about. How it was about God and me. About His heart and mine. How I needed to "Be still and know that He was God." It was not the organ; not the music nor the microphone. Not the stained-glass windows. It was not the worshippers' attire. This rich lesson gave me new joy. I lost my worship critique! Once again, I experienced God's loving lessons. It was to be God and me.

Lunch after church was another lesson on false and inflated anticipation. In their lovely home, I had expected my own traditional hot Sunday dinner meal. I had so missed that with only cold sandwiches daily. Instead, as we sat down to a pretty table with real fine china plates and cups, I was served lunch, in typical Australian style for a Sunday. A cold cooked meat log was plattered in the center of the lovely table and tender slices beautifully placed on my plate along with breads and hard-boiled egg wedges. Some salad veggies made the flowered china plate really appetizing. It was the grape season and there were many colors of them offered there. The meal was totally delicious. Just surprising. Just unexpected. And just not hot!

A really special treat ended the day though as we sat in the living room and, in lovely Aussie style, were served hot tea with milk and lemon. For the first time in my life I had a chocolate mint placed alongside this delicate china cup on the china saucer. I felt like the

Queen! It was such a fitting end to this unpredictable Sunday.

In the book of Proverbs is a wonderful lesson. Again, now learned many times and with worship especially. "Many are the plans of man, but God's purposes prevail." It was so true for me. I had plans. I had my own many plans for this day and worship. But thanks be to God, He has purposes. I am blessed because of this truth.

Chapter 9

The Mesmerizing Mongoose

Our mission assignment in the South Pacific Fiji Islands was rich and varied. Our work changed daily with the needs and with the availability of supply and service. One day, Bob was sitting on a low wall with a young Fijian, Joe, basking in the sunshine at the Church of the Nazarene Boys' Ranch site. *What work needs might I be able to help with?* Such a lovely place it was, set in the heavy timber of that area, close to many groves of the precious hardwoods so common there. Beautiful woods were available for specialized furniture making or decorative needs. These were rare and very valuable. The rich tropical soil and sun along with much needed rain made this a productive place. This niche though was set up as a special place of care and rehab ministry for boys. The local Nazarene Church had noted this need with so many street boys in the town. Footloose and alone for one reason or another, too many were sunken deeply in the drug culture.

Joe shared that, though dorm rooms had been completed for housing, more construction was needed. Some agriculture had been set up to support this good program. The plan included loving care, counseling and work study there in a Christian setting. God had raised up talented Fijians to lead in this good work.

As Bob looked out to one side, he saw the manmade pond Joe had shared about, where shrimp farming had been started. This would help keep the Ranch self-supporting and give the boys work skills too. Down below us were great, long chicken houses for the main support of the work. In these several buildings the boys would feed young chicks until they became adults, right on to meat marketing time. The Ranch had already acquired good contracts for this productive economic vision.

Over this peaceful scene Bob kept hearing sudden sounds from Joe. He loudly clapped every so often but for no obvious reason. Curious, Bob asked him about it. Joe pointed down to the chicken houses and told this interesting story. "See, down there? That is the young chicks housing where we start them before they can be sent on to the meat producing housing. You can see them running around inside the wire-sided walls. The traditional chicken wire down there is in small octagonal shapes. It lets in sun and fresh air as it keeps the chicks safe inside. See them running back and forth? They are so interested and curious about what they can see outside." He shared how this curiosity becomes a huge danger for them.

Joe continued to relate that long ago many snakes plagued the Fiji Islands. The natives from India, who were brought here as indentured servants to work the sugar cane fields, were naturally afraid of them. But they remembered a solution for this problem back in their home country of India: the common mongoose. This small, furry, rodent-like, carnivorous mammal with its long fluffy tail loved to eat snakes. It was known to charm Indian cobras and kill them. Why not bring some over here to solve this problem? This seemingly good idea took hold and soon the local snakes had a new enemy. But the mongoose multiplied and became a pest as is so often the case with this type of imported plan. Now here at the Boys Ranch, with its good meat poultry program, they had become a real danger to the young chicks.

The mongoose found out that he could not get into the wire fencing to the tasty chicks, but was especially clever and took advantage of this strong curiosity of the young birds. He had used his skills in India to tempt the cobras, so it might work here too, he thought. He would parade alongside this outer wire fencing, taunting and inviting the chicks. He was a showman! He would dance! He would sway! He strode boldly back and forth in front of the small birds eyes, his long fluffy tail waving temptingly. It made these young ones ponder just what wonder was out there, and what if we could get out? What fun we might have with him...hmmm. So it seemed.

The wire would not let their bodies out though. What could they do? It was all so desirable and so interesting and so wonderful in the small chicks' eyes. *Perhaps we could just poke our heads through the wire-holes. We can't get our bodies out but maybe we can get a little closer. Let's do it!* And so, when tempted, chicks yielded to the tempter. They would stick their small heads out though the wire in front of the swaying mongoose...and snatch! Bite! Grab! That chick was headless and the mongoose had his lunch!

To save as many as they could when they were sighted, the Boys Ranch staff would clap their hands loudly to scare away the mongoose. They would be able to save several that way. So, as the sounds of clapping was heard often through the day, Bob was intrigued with this story and the obvious lesson.

In the coming years, when we were asked to share missions with children, Bob would often tell this dramatic story. He could act as eager to get out of the fencing as a chick. He could be a mongoose and sway and dance with charm. He would tell them about the tantalizing tempter that the small chicks saw through the protective fencing. How it pulled them to want to be with that mongoose and in that very interesting outside world! He shared with them about the needed fencing and how it would save their lives from a terrible death if they would just stay inside. Yet, how often the pull to do wrong would make them stick their heads out. That one small thing to do, just that one time. Just for a minute perhaps. But no! It was exactly what the mongoose had planned.

    He then shared how this was just what the evil one, Satan, has planned for each of us. He wants to tempt us and then to take and use our very life. Satan wants us for his own uses and enjoyment. But if we have put our trust and belief in Jesus, we are a part of His own safely cared for flock. We are in His good care. His kind of fencing is important and good in His plan for our safety. Jesus' great love for us means He wants to protect us if we choose to obey Him. Such good care Jesus gives us if we just stay with Him in his own good fencing for our lives. While Bob often told this lesson to children, it is for us all. Let none of us listen to that old mongoose, Satan. Right?

Chapter 10

Fiji Island Friends

We were in the Fiji Islands in the South Pacific on missionary assignment and had just met the Indian pastor of our Fiji Indian Church of the Nazarene. As was our custom, we loved having people in our home, sharing food, hearing their stories, and enjoying new experiences. I prepared a dinner of Mexican food and invited the pastor and his family to join us one evening. It was an interesting start to the meal as I explained all about the menu. There were chicken or beef tacos; beef burritos; tortillas, hand made by me; salsa, hot or mild; chicken enchiladas; etc. It had been such fun to get it all ready. As I had somewhat known the people of India and their love of fiery hot curry, I felt this food might just fit in with their taste buds. After all, isn't it really a great part of the American food choices? I saw it as a shared cultural experience with them.

A pause just after Bob's blessing was filled in by the words of our pastoral guest. He said that while he was now a Christian, he still held to one of his Hindu traditions, that of not eating beef. He explained that in India in the Hindu religion, the cow is considered their Mother as she gives them their food staples of milk, cheese, and yogurt. They would not consider eating the flesh of this Mother of theirs. Though, he explained, he does not worship the cow, he still does not eat its meat. He asked us if we would eat our Mother who had nursed us with her milk. "Of course not," we clearly stated. He quickly mentioned that the rest of his family loved beef and ate it heartily with his blessing. They would be happy with this meal. I saw this was so as I looked at the beaming faces of his lovely wife, his grown son seated with his fiancé, and his two teenaged boys. I immediately apologized and was glad that in the kitchen I still had more chicken to quickly make up into extra dishes Pastor would enjoy with no discomfort. Thus, we all set into this great time of fellowship. During this festive meal and later in the long evening to come, we sipped our tea and listened to the wonderful history and experiences of this godly family which had crossed our paths so blessedly. We loved the way that it seems natural for these islanders, when asked, to give their past histories with deep and colorful detail. We love the practice here too, that time is of no concern. There is no rush to get on and out and leave friends quickly. Thus, we settled into comfortable living room seating, with open hearts and minds as Pastor began to share.

The local, national, Fijians in these hundreds of islands lived contentedly mainly from the surrounding sea and from coconuts. These food sources were seasonally worked, and their lifestyle was casually lived with healthy food. They were fishermen and agriculturalists. They knew how to dry and preserve both of these crops. A coconut palm would grow on even a small dot of earth-covered coral out in the seas surrounding these South Pacific isles. Each family had enough. They also harvested and dried them for trading on other islands. They produced coconut oil and milk by shredding and squeezing the fresh pulp. This added labor to the preparation of delicious food, and this natural healing oil beautifully glossed their skin and hair. They lived with the surrounding sea and the many kinds of fish that were readily available. Their outrigger canoes and special nets worked so well along with innate skills developed over the centuries. Because of the tropical breezes, and in the equatorial heat. work was done casually, and rest was a needed part of every day. It all made for a slower pace of living and working.

The one national blight was the continued historical tradition of cannibalism. Eating the flesh of conquered enemies after tribal fighting was meant to strengthen the warriors. In earlier years, when the London Missionary Society was at its height of evangelism, these islands were covered with prayer and missionaries. God moved and a rich harvest for the

Gospel abounded with changed hearts and with churches springing up all over. One miraculous, large event was the immediate and permanent ending of the practice of cannibalism. It totally stopped when Christianity came into hearts and lives. These new Christians became missionaries themselves, traveling in their outriggers over the seas to other islands spreading the Good News. Spiritual growth abounded in these South Pacific waters.

Then, about three hundred years ago, sudden massive changes came to their world. These islands, along with others in the South Pacific, could not escape the development of the world of ships crossing their seas, and the startling discovery of new lands and possibilities. It was soon seen that their land and breezes would be good for the planting of sugar cane. Surely there would be a strong market for processed sugar in India and other parts of the developed world. But sugar cane needs a lot of manual labor, a multitude of strong backs. It meant that human hands were needed and the new plantation owners sought for many.

This labor was not in the local population with their casual style of working, yet, a source was soon seen. A large labor force existed in heavily populated India, and soon shiploads of strong men arrived from there to do this work. Those days were hard, and changes came not only to the local islanders but to these shiploads of Indian indentured servants. Now, an ocean away from familiar customs, they lost their caste system, they lost family, they lost promises of wealth and security. Yet, the plantation owners found the perfect workforce in these men from India. They had a mind to work, they could stand the heat, and they were used to the activity from working back in India, many in sugar cane fields there. The cane business expanded quickly and more and more workers were brought over from India with the same weak promises. Soon, plantations with sugar cane fields covered the land. The manual labor of Indian workers continued to be needed. More and more were imported.

    The local Fijians did not fit into this new kind of manual labor so intense and fixed. Yet, as the years passed, the national Fijians adjusted to the business activity of these new families from India. They liked to buy the fabric sold in these small Indian shops, or in the arms of sellers along the streets. And they loved the imported trinkets and supplies, pots and pans and many other items now sold in the stores run by these good business people fairly new to the islands. As in so many other places the blend of newness became familiar and worked well for both the new and old populations. The people of India valued education and schools soon filled with eager learners who did not mind sitting in classes nor the endless studying required. They advanced quickly. The blending of this new and the old soon seemed natural and both cultures fit well into the development of the country. With the passing of centuries, both claimed Fiji as their own.

The native Fiji islanders became prime workers in the expanding tourist industry, being well-able to serve. Their easy ways fit well into the many foreign visitors' lives who came to enjoy these blue waters, lazy tropical breezes and wonderful food. They developed the recreational and resort businesses so well. They became leaders in government and business as well using their great skills in quiet conversation and diplomacy.

As these islands were made known to the rest of the world, many Christian groups were glad to come to renew and add to the initial work of those who had labored here long ago. Wonderful spiritual growth came to lives in this lovely mix of nations. Now, after some three hundred years, the Indian ethnic group had grown to become around fifty percent of the population. A good balance seemed to occur in all areas. Many denominations came to serve, and the Church of the Nazarene was one of these sending a missionary. They found welcome in Fiji national lives and planted many churches. Nazarene pastors were trained as a local Bible College was begun. In time, national leaders bloomed in these quiet people and grace abounded in spiritual development. God worked His ways in hearts and people were blessed.

Still, the Indian people had not yet specifically been addressed by our church. Coming so long ago to these islands, most had lost their Hindu religious traditions and were adrift spiritually. The Church of the Nazarene saw this need and began to plant churches and prepare pastors for this particular culture and language. They still had their own way of dressing in lovely, flowing saris. They continued to prepare the hot curried foods they loved. Along with their unusual stringed instruments and songs they had hung on to much of their past.

The Church began to pray for God's leading in this. Now this evening, around our table we were meeting an answer to that very prayer. We eagerly listened as Pastor now began to share how God started to move in his and his family's lives. Early in their marriage they were practicing Hindus, strongly involved in the high end of it in Hari Krishna beliefs. They relied heavily on the multitude of prayers with the use of many beads, done in a very precise manner. Their dietary needs were specific and tightly adhered to. Following these were supposed to bring peace, health, and good luck to them. They had good employment and education and were content with their young son. His wife's sister often invited them to her Christian church, but they were not interested. They felt they had already achieved the highly desired "good luck" prayed for and promised.

One day his wife began to have extreme pain in her foot. It soon caused her to miss work in the lab where she was a technician. They could find no help for it medically. Her husband boldly told her she probably was not doing her beads correctly nor praying often enough. Perhaps she was not eating the right things. That must be the problem. He often told her, "See, I am doing all these things right and I have no pain nor problems. See?"

    Her sister kept inviting her to church and sharing how her pastor would pray for her foot and God could heal her. In time, because of the continued pain and loss of work, she finally, reluctantly, agreed to attend. One Sunday she took their young five-year-old son along and went with her sister. In the service, at the healing prayer time, she and the small son went forward to the altar. The pastor's prayer over her was in the name of Jesus, for Satan's defeat and for her healing. Instantly, God, in Jesus' name, did just that. Right there and then He healed her foot and the pain left immediately. What joy and rejoicing there was. She gave her heart fully to Jesus and came home a new woman with a healed foot.

    Her husband felt he obviously had to accept this miracle but was still skeptical. Though his wife now attended church, he still did not. One day soon after this, his foot was in great pain and in the next few days it became just like his wife's problem had been before. It hurt excruciatingly! Though he continued to rely on his Hari Krishna methods to heal, it was to no avail. His wife had quickly been able to resume her good employment in the hospital lab, but now his highly valued work as cab driver was in jeopardy. Soon the pain escalated to the point that he could no longer drive nor work at all. He sat miserably at home with his foot elevated.

One day he was in such pain he cried out to his young boy. "Son, what is Daddy going to do? How will I ever get better?"

That moment his son remembered what he had seen the pastor do for his Mother. He lay his little hand on his daddy's foot and his young voice prayed aloud, "In Jesus' name I command you to be gone, Satan, and now Daddy, you be healed!" His small son's innocent, faith-filled prayer reached God. As had happened with his wife, now too his own healing, right there in his own home, was immediate and miraculous.

He rejoiced and immediately recognized Jesus' work in his own body. He too became a believer in Him. Now the family was one in faith and blessing. He decided to attend church with his wife and son the next Sunday. Oddly, though, that Sunday there was a dismissal of the present pastor and conflict was all over the congregation. Upon arriving home, they found their home had been robbed! With these two events, from Satan's store of hindrances, it still did not deter this family from wanting to serve God. They started to listen to some cassettes they found with Scriptural sermons. They began to read the Bible and grew in wisdom from the Word. God was speaking to him and he was sensing a call to share his faith somewhere, somehow. In God's own perfect timing, the Nazarene missionary met this called Indian man and sensed God's answer to prayer in him. With training and growth, Pastor began to lead this Indian congregation to become firmly established. Soon a lovely church building was erected in their own Indian/Fijian community of homes. His pastoral leading was bearing fruit. Certainly, a circuitous route but often the way God works. With Him all things are possible.

After dinner and this testimony of God in this great family's lives, we were so moved and blessed. We rejoiced and prayed together. How good to see what we had seen God do in our own personal lives, His links in a chain, now produced also in this good Indian family. How good to see answered prayer before us. How very good!

A few weeks later, we witnessed others of this pastor's family being baptized far out in the ocean looking out and beyond these islands, testifying to Jesus' work of death and resurrection in their lives.

When Bob saw that their church did not have a cross, it was his privilege to make one out of beautiful wood, stain and polish it, and deliver it to that church. The men had been awaiting Bob's coming and rushed out to unload it almost before the vehicle stopped! Taking it right in and hanging it up at the front of the sanctuary was a joy to see. Jesus' empty cross. Now a testimony for all to see in yet another culture.

Chapter 11

COME, NOW IS THE TIME TO WORSHIP

SCENE 3

After one of our usual four-year assignments, it was time for our furlough back to the States. We had been invited to speak in Europe on the way, so we headed for London, and Rome, along with a speaking tour of our Nazarene churches in Germany also. Sharing our dear Papua New Guinean mission work was always a pleasure for us. We looked into travel plans. Wonderfully, it was learned that the "Round the World" trip tickets would actually be less expensive than the usual ones of just home and return to the field. So it was decided. Accepting these European church experiences would be wonderfully new to us, plus we would be able to do a bit of touring. Soon we were off to arrive at London's Heathrow Airport.

We both had strong desires to see some great places along our way. One, for Bob, was to run on the Great Wall and in our passing through Beijing, China, he had the joy of doing just that. For myself, I wanted to see the great Canterbury Cathedral, in Kent, England, which Saint Augustine founded and where the Church of England is centered. Not only had its history called to me, but also its intrigue and tragedy. I had recently read the history of Archbishop Thomas Becket and his vicious murder within the Cathedral's walls All this pulled me towards the Eastern side of England. Speaking engagements did press us in time and dates, but in checking these and the map we saw it as only a six-hour drive from the West of England to the East. So we said, "Let's go to Canterbury Cathedral."

We had just seen a lot of London with all its pomp. We enjoyed Devonshire tea, gazed at Buckingham Palace, and had Sunday worship in St. Paul's Cathedral where Prince Charles and Princess Di were wed. To top all this, we had stood among the loving, cheering crowds along the street as the Queen passed us in her open carriage in honor of her birthday. The time-worn stone in the many towering buildings pulled our gaze upward many times. Their age alone was striking. In America, we think of an antique as around one hundred years old, but in the U.K. they start to honor structures at around one thousand years of age. So, we were ready for my longed-for visit to Canterbury, all awash in its particular history.

We arrived there on a Friday evening to another of my dreams, a lovely Bed and Breakfast. The pink and white satin was not on Bob's list but was nevertheless outstanding, as was breakfast the next morning. The table was full of antique crystal and silver set upon linen, on which was served wonderful English food. Stewed prunes, a childhood memory of my own; new items such as hot grilled tomatoes and mushrooms; eggs with toast points; rashers, which is bacon; and gabion, which we call ham. All this was served with warm, fresh breads, real butter, and bright, raspberry preserves. What a start to our day.

Soon we were off to the Cathedral nearby. What a sight! The very strength of its huge stones! We faced the tallest of its five towers reaching 236 feet into the sky. Here is the mother church of the Church of England, the Anglican Communion. I caught my breath. What a history.

This had all begun less than six hundred years after the death of Christ, when Pope Gregory the Great of Rome, known to be a bit aggressive, sent a very reluctant priest, Augustine by name, as a missionary to take Christianity to pagan England. Augustine was bishop in Rome and would have preferred to stay there. But he reluctantly submitted to authority and, taking forty priests with him in a wooden boat, sailed for this remote northern piece of land. He landed in an area called Canterbury in 597 A.D., met the pagan King Ethelbert, and was given land and allowed to stay.

In time, along with his missionary work and converts, he began to build this magnificent church near his original landing site. Construction of the current structure began in 1060 AD, and was finished in 1834 AD, almost 800 years in the making. In time it became not only the Mother Church, but a famous pilgrimage destination. Now, standing in front of its towering spires, huge doors, and ancient age-marked gray stone, was inspiring.

As we stepped into the nave with its eighty-foot vaulted ceiling rising above us, I was so glad we had come this particular weekend. It was to be the celebration and reenactment of St. Augustine's landing and special services would be held. We were not aware of this until we arrived and had observed some happenings when driving along the lake shore. An old wooden boat had landed there, offloading a corps of priests with pomp and prayers walking behind a huge cross carried in front of the entourage. History repeated!

Now within the nave, we saw even more signs of celebration. Church women dressed in plain gray gowns with long aprons were mopping the stone floors and steps. Footstep-worn dips showed hundreds of years of wear and made me ponder. Every corner was filled with beautiful and majestic eight-foot-tall floral arrangements. It was then that we found out about the events to come in this celebrated building. Today, Saturday, was preparation for Sunday which would celebrate a worship service open to all. Then on Monday, the actual historical landing date would be noted with a special invitation-only worship service in the Cathedral, officiated by the Archbishop himself. The special guest for that event was Prince Charles. This would complete the week of celebrating this pivotal historic religious event. We certainly would attend tomorrow for the open worship. Freshly arriving from our more primitive Papua New Guinea, my heart so looked forward to worship within this place.

Continuing our walk through, we had our own quiet pilgrimage. With almost no one around, we were able to just absorb the strength, beauty, and history of this place at our own pace. It touched my heart as I lay my hands on the aged stone. With hundreds of candles flickering there, we knelt and lit one for our son, Paul, in the war and we read the plaques with the honored martyrs' names, even one who had been in Papua New Guinea. It was a wondrous circuit of stark loveliness, candlelight, and floral scent. Hushed and thoughtful, we whispered our way along.

Within these precious walls, we finally came to a very special memorial. In front of us was the very place where Thomas Becket was murdered. I had read of how at that time he was the Archbishop of Canterbury, head of that church for the world. This was the same time that the wicked King Henry the Eighth had come into power. The king, in envy and hatred, had made himself head of the Church of England so he could annul his own marriage and marry another. He had not been able to force Archbishop Thomas Becket into doing this for him, nor would the Archbishop condone his taking over the Church. Thus King Henry the Eighth hated him vilely. Traditional history noted that one day the king shouted out, "Will no one save me from this wretched man?", meaning Thomas Becket and his godly stand. Four of his men grabbed their swords and stormed the cathedral. There inside, they found the Archbishop and brutally cut him down. Now, in our very sacred walk, we came upon this small spot, with its small bronze plaque, by a small table, to mark this great man's martyrdom. It made me weep. Bob and I took this quiet and private time to reflect on life and death and our own commitment to God.

This mood stayed with us and carried us to the Sunday worship service the next morning. The Cathedral was not just a tourist attraction, but a regular church used by the locals for their regular Sunday services. As we arrived, we sensed the presence of God. The Cathedral was awash in candlelight and chairs were set in ways new to us-in rows all facing a single central aisle. The ornate preaching pulpit was raised above us at the head of this aisle. We had front row seats and, providentially, a local companion. He whispered a quiet welcome to us. The service began with a procession down the aisle in front of us. A swaying incense sensor was carried by a young clergyman. Our companion quietly shared that some might be bothered by the scent and smoke and I should feel free to cover my face as this came alongside. Instead, I found it a lovely introduction to worship. The fragrance, the candles, the walls and the high nave filled me. I was lifted above myself, learning about worship. Finally, it became just God and me.

As the service continued, a small lectern was placed in the aisle in front of us. A Bible was placed upon it and from it the Gospel was read to us all. I'm not sure why our helper knew this was all new to us but he leaned in to say this was done to place the written, spoken, Word-being the very living Word, Christ Himself-right in our midst. I knew too, this was exactly where He was needed and wanted to be. It was such a wondrous, visual, preparation for worship. I felt Him there.

We had known there would be communion and had assumed we would sit quietly as others partook. But we were all invited to share if we were Believers. What joy it was to reverently stand and file past the priest, dip our bread into the cup, and do this "in Remembrance of Him". Seated again, we were ready for the preaching. Since the Archbishop would preside the following day, this service was given to missions with a special speaker. The head of the Division on Missions for the Church brought the message. He spoke in part of an overbearing pope, Gregory the Great, and a reluctant missionary, St. Augustine, and how God used them both. How He took man's many plans and made it fit His own specific purposes. How it had grown and now we sat in this place and at this time to reflect and see these Christian results.

As I listened, I sensed my own missionary call all over again. I accepted it joyfully. I worshipped. It truly became between God and me. Perhaps I had finally learned this truth and had now finally sensed his invitation to…

COME, NOW IS THE TIME TO WORSHIP.

Chapter 12

Port Moresby: Painful Purpose

After almost two years in the high Schrader Mountain ranges of Papua New Guinea, and nearly finishing the airstrip there, we were asked by the Church to temporarily fill in for the missionaries in the capital city, Port Moresby, way down on the coast. Their furlough/home assignment had been arranged for the next four months and now they were ready to take this needed break. It was exciting for us too. We had spent our recent days with no roads, no traffic lights, no businesses, no phones, and no stores, (well one small shack selling warm Coke and small bags of rice). No computers, no regular, powerful electricity but only solar, and no personal responsibility for daily labor management. This would be different and a physical change. We looked forward to it.

So now, here we were to care for this city church property, assist the pastoral students in English Bible College study, encourage the several pastors in the area with helpful meetings, and do the financial business for the church districts and the country. It would be new but, as was usual for us, we expected the differences to be therapeutic. We loved our nearly twenty years in PNG and had found that new challenges usually ended up being a blessing.

As we overlapped with the leaving missionaries by a couple of weeks, we were oriented to our most important work. For Bob that was keeping the office open for pastors, planning for their meetings, and seeing to the compound property management and rental of apartments not needed for Bible College students. I was quickly trained for the district and national financial work, mostly done via computer—all brand new to me. Pastors needed pay sent to their accounts, mission bills were to be paid, country taxes were sent to government receivers, and many other needs met. I was so ignorant about technology. My trainer was very good; her notes were detailed. She started with, "Press the blue button." And we were off! She wrote down each and every move and tab for me to follow. I practiced with her eye on me and it all seemed to be going well. This training time before they left, though beneficial, was short and hence troublesome for both Bob and me.

All too quickly we found ourselves alone with this new work. We did our best to find our way and fit in and do what we needed to do. Bob met the pastors and encouraged them the best he knew how. He tried to use the office phone bank, though it was complicated with voicemail and other buttons he found hard to learn. Having spent the last many months on a tractor while building the remote mountain airstrip, this now seemed too much for him. Also, his work history being in maintenance, he had never been asked to lead pastors in studies or gatherings. With his quiet and retiring demeanor he found it difficult and stressful. Bob's office was in the maintenance building and mine in the nearby home. We were trying to cope. Though working apart on the compound, we often met for coffee and shared feelings of inadequacy.

  Some of our first pains were the cultural aspects and change. In the mountains we spoke only the Melanesian Pidgin English which the nationals there spoke along with their local languages. But here, in the city, English was most commonly spoken, and we even felt the newness of that. Formerly, everyone visited with each other as they walked by or just came and sat on our verandah for a cuppa and chat. Now here, they appeared busily scheduled. Many were on their way to work, or to town or market and seemed hurried and distant. We found it very seldom that they even casually connected. Our verandah, elevated above the street, stayed empty. Pastors were scattered, with their churches across the city and out at area plantations and had to take a bus to attend meetings. Thus, Bob seldom saw them at all. He felt so inadequate.

He put ads in the paper to rent the apartments available. He happily got interested people scheduled for appointments. He would sit on the verandah swing awaiting their time to come, holding required papers in his hand. But they did not come! There on the verandah he waited and waited, to no avail. He learned that people here would most often say they were coming just to please you but had no intention of doing so. Of course, not letting your know hurt him. After many times like this, he lost all trust in city people and felt despair in this new job. Though some appointments did work out, most hurt his sense of trust. Once more he felt he could not do this job!

For myself, I had to really focus on the computer work and found it hard. The work was so exacting and important. Error could cause deep problems and it made me tense and apprehensive. I really could not do this! It was further complicated by the fact that we were used to the cool high mountain weather and now, almost on the equator and at sea level, we suffered from the heat and humidity. We learned to move more slowly, sit when needed, and drink lots of liquids. We did have air conditioning for our bedroom, which helped with sleep.

The city was rife with criminal activity. We had become spoiled by the ways of the peaceful mountain tribes. These city *rascals* were always trying to get into our well-fenced property and take whatever they could find. Even in daytime you locked the house doors—

even when you were inside. Our nighttime security man was wonderful and had a large German shepherd dog to work with him as he checked the dark, well-fenced perimeter. One night he found a hole cut in the woven wire and before he could stop the dog, it had run out and chased the *rascals* away. Later, limping back inside, he had been deeply slashed by a machete and his hip badly wounded and bleeding. This was devastating to see. A veterinarian decided he would not make it and had to be put down. Such a loss, and such a painful time for Bob. Again, because he sensed this failure, he felt he was not doing his job well.

    I needed to regularly do bank business and also get cash for my work. Even as a capital city this was still just a small town, so driving to the bank was a short trip. It had been robbed the day before I went one time but still it was just *par for the course*, as they say. God helped me to never be afraid. We had one traffic light to deal with. Bob had not driven, other than the tractor, for two years. Hard! And on the "other" side of the road too. His mountain tractor driving had not been like this! More stress for the both of us. Airport trips were a part of it all too. Meeting international visitors connected with the mission, coming and going, was a treat for me, but with the very erratic flight schedules, it often meant long hours of waiting in the terminal.

    We had a TV with VCR but with all our years in PNG we had never used one nor even inserted a video. We tried, and after much frustration, succeeded and sometimes were able to spend time in the evening relaxing. The tropical beauty of the coast and the many blooming flowers all lent to our day. We found being close by the ocean interesting, with its ships coming and going. These bits and pieces helped soothe, but still our spirits were filled with our own sense of inability and the continual question, "Why were we sent here when we are so inadequate?"

These first short painful weeks were escalated by sudden personal trauma. Our son phoned to relate that Bob's dad was dying. We knew he had been in the nursing home but had no idea it was this serious and so unexpected. Bob tried to talk with his dad on the phone but could only hear his sad heavy breathing. The next day his earthly life ended, and he entered his heavenly one. We had always known his dad's godliness and love of the Lord and were looking forward to this for his sake. Now, 10,000 miles away, for Bob it was hard to bear. His grief was deep and lonely. With no one else to take our place, we were unable to return for the funeral. Here there was no comforting missionary family. We were so alone. We did not have much emotional energy for each other either, as we had too often focused on our own pain and solitary needs born in this new place and time. We were all alone. Grief-stricken. Unable.

A few days later, Bob was in his office when the phone rang. He could hear our daughter, Laurie, on the phone. He so longed to talk with her and tried to answer. In his nervous state it seemed that all the phone buttons and pieces just would not let him connect. He heard it finally go to voice mail and her comforting, sweet words melted him. Frustrated, he still could not talk to her. He could not get the line open and soon it was only her, "Love you, Dad. Goodbye", followed by that sad and empty dial tone. Standing there beside the phone, somehow it seemed to be the last straw. He came into the house and I felt his pain as he leaned over the kitchen sink weeping.

He cried out in his spirit, "God, did I do something wrong? It that the reason I was sent here where I cannot do anything? Where I don't know how to do the things I am asked to do? Where I have never done these things before? Where I am a failure?" We held each other as we shared tears.

The next morning, we did as we have always done these years in PNG. We had our devotions. We loved reading the Bible. Praying for our children back in the US gave us a connection with them and a connection with God for our own daily lives. Here in these strained times though, it had become dutiful, more of a habitual ritual. But still…we got our coffee, hot chocolate, toast and, as usual, sitting propped up with pillows in bed, we opened God's Word. We had been reading the Bible through and had now come to the Old Testament book of Nehemiah. Of course, we had read this in times past, but today as Bob started reading through those first few verses our eyes were shockingly opened!

Here was Nehemiah, the King's personal cupbearer, with clean, neat, well-manicured hands, being asked by God to go and finish building the stone wall of Jerusalem! There is no record that he was a former contractor or that he had any experience with crumbled stone! But he obeyed. He went! Here too we read of a perfumer being asked to do the wall repair in front of his home. He, who had formerly worked with oils and tiny flasks and scents, also did this new thing that he was being asked to do. Next were the two goldsmiths who had been used to small links and chains and sensitive fingers and a clean, tidy, shop. They too were asked to rebuild, using huge rough stones and getting dirty in the process. They responded to this new task. They went to work. Then we read lastly about the man with only daughters being asked to help too. These girls certainly did not have any experience outside of their father's kitchen and home. Yet they also went to work with their dad. All these people did what they were asked to do. All was new and different work. All was difficult and frustrating for them for sure. All were totally inexperienced.

Soon there in that morning bed, we read the wonderful verse following which says, "And the wall was finished! And the people worshipped." God just poured that Scripture into our hearts that morning. Here we saw it all! We saw ourselves. Here were these others, totally without the needed skills, being asked to do what they did not know how to do in hard places with added physical pain. Who were we to question God and His ways? We were lifted by these examples! Together we rejoiced in this new insight and leading and felt at peace. We were grateful for the "dutiful" devotions and the obedience even when we did not "feel" like doing it. God had led us to this Scriptural lesson. We were not the only ones ever asked by God to do what they did not know how to do. In this way, God, not we, would get the credit in the end. God built the wall in Jerusalem, and He would accomplish all He wanted done here in Port Moresby by us because of His strength. We praised Him.

With quieted hearts we settled in and peacefully did all we were asked to do. Bob learned to answer the phone, I learned to press keys carefully, and we did not make any major mistakes. We felt closer to the pastors and families, arranging gatherings for them all together. Students prepared local food for us and we felt their friendship even over the years to come. We were also able, just by our being there, to be instrumental in the purchase of land and the building of a church in a strategic area of the city. We saw pain there but also the promises of God.

So we too saw "the wall was finished and the people worshipped" written all over our lives.

Chapter 13

Just Enough

For our first two years of retirement, Bob volunteered to accept the Church's request to finish the grass airstrip high in the Schrader Ranges of Papua New Guinea. Just thinking of those future hours of tractor driving there brought him joy. All those years ago in South Dakota it had been his favorite farming job. Just driving on and on across the acres, seeing the soil turn over behind him with the gulls swooping down for worms was peaceful and fulfilling. Now, for him to consider this new volunteer assignment from the Church of the Nazarene would be just what he wanted to be doing in retirement.

Thus, we moved into our small yellow bamboo home situated alongside a nearby airstrip to be as close as possible to his work on up and over the range in Gebrau. This whole area was ministered to by our church with healthy growth. Many young men were in training for the pastorate and they joyously ran the trails to share Christ and teach and preach the Gospel. This completed strip would add to this ministry and mission to the national people.

The strip where Bob would work was at the summit and had been started some time before. For guest accommodation a small room had been added to the pastor's home thirty minutes below the mountaintop. This would be Bob's bedroom for his stay there. He would lay his sleeping bag on the woven bamboo slats and try to get comfortable. They had a short-wave radio for outside contact with the mission hospital and other airstrips. This was a common and necessary way to communicate in the many mountain areas without roads. This mountain top was where Bob would spend his days during the week.

A group of young men arrived at our home each Monday morning to fill and carry the fuel for the tractor. They literally ran singing as they crossed back up the trail with their heavy loads tied to their backs with vines. Wesley, whom Bob called his "angel", was assigned to get Bob safely through the mudslide and rain damaged trails to his destination weekly. Bob used to say, "He guided my climb upward and slowed my slide downward." So, each Monday morning, this group cheerfully set off together. I always felt a loss as he left as I had never been alone like this before in my married life, for days at time. Yet I knew it was God's calling and Bob was really happy to do this work.

After three to five hours of mountain trekking, they arrived at Gebrau. Along the way Bob rested only by leaning against a tree. When I asked him why he did not sit down to more completely rest he answered, "If I had done that, I would never have been able to get back up!" This same trek, though a bit more downhill, was repeated as he returned to me each Friday with the same "angel". I was always glad to see Bob again and after sending Wesley off with our gratitude, we were now alone. With the porch swing ready, his muddy shoes off, and with a cold Coke in his hand, we rested together. These weeks went by peacefully and as the work continued, Bob began to feel a sense of accomplishment. It seemed though, at times he was "digging with a teaspoon," he said. Yet as time passed, he could see the mountains coming down and the valleys filling to level it up. *Yes, it would finally get done.*

Cowboy, the *boskrew*, or foreman, was an able site leader and kept the large group of local men working at a good pace to do what extensive manual work was needed. They would undercut the outcropping mountain soil with their long, strong, digging sticks, and when it fell, they carried it off on burlap coffee bags strung on long poles. Wheelbarrows were scarce. Bit by bit the earth was moved along with Bob on the tractor and scraper doing his part.

Thus two years went by. During that time other interested expatriates came, trekking across to see the development and cheer the work on. Some marveled at Bob's ability to merely get back and forth to the site as he was over sixty-five years of age. One exhausted mountain trekking young man said, "All that kept me going was seeing that old man up ahead of me, still moving upward!" Our son Carl visited and was awed at the immense work done by so many with so little. A photographer took to the trails once and the film shows the work done so well in one accord and little in the way of equipment. One filmed scene reveals a dozen men with their digging sticks thrust into the ground as pry bars in synchronized movement. They removed a huge tangled clump of bamboo, roots and all, from the site. They chanted in song as they worked, giving encouragement and rhythm to each other. Bob saw many such scenes in his time there and was blessed by this strong commitment to the completion of this great local need—an airstrip! The sheer natural beauty was awesome too. The bright New Guinea impatiens growing so tall all around the construction area lifted him daily. Smoke rising from Manamp, a volcano out in the Pacific Ocean was often visible. Views like this moved him.

This area produced the most wonderful Arabica coffee and was prized by the country's international coffee connections. Getting it to them was the problem. Usually the local ninety-pound women carried the one hundred pound bags on their heads down the same trail Bob traveled weekly, to the airstrip alongside our bamboo home. Then a radio message would call in a plane to take it out for sale. The trail was always subject to the rainy weather making slippery footpaths for their bare feet. Fallen trees along the trek often blocked the usual paths. This coffee was the prime national export and a cash crop for the nationals. They needed this for school fees for their children, for medical care not available locally, or purchasing items not grown in their limited, high-mountain gardens. Importantly, too, cash was necessary for the bride price needed for acquiring wives and pigs. This was vital for doing business in PNG. It was interesting to see this chain of events, so difficult yet so common to them, done without complaint and with seeming ease. A continual marvel to us.

As the assigned two years passed and the strip's completion became obvious, Bob looked forward to our home assignment and the change of scene. Many times, he wondered if the strip's completion would ever happen. Yet daily, a "spoonful at a time," he now saw it before his eyes. Excitement built among the workers also. One day, Cowboy told Bob that they were planning a big PNG feast to celebrate the now-completed strip and Bob would be the honored guest. It would be a great time. Everyone in the community would bring something—perhaps a chicken or a pig, sweet potatoes or some taro roots, or the local greens. Then he notified Bob that he could too, and hinted that he should bring a contribution even as the honored guest. *"Perhaps cow meat?"* Since we did not know any ranchers, had seen no cattle, nor did we raise pigs, nor chickens, nor grew gardens there, we wondered how we would work this all out.

In our regular letter to our Sunday school class back home, we shared our ministry and needs. They had followed our lives in PNG and were happy with us for these final days of this work there. They read of the commitment and the coming party and all that it entailed. A couple of men there had the idea that they would love to take on Bob's contribution, the cow meat! Cheerfully they sent money for that part of the feast. When Bob gave it to Cowboy, he was naturally quite pleased.

Finally, the Feast Day arrived and as Bob walked that last bit up to the top of the site he noted cooking fires all over the area around the new strip. Smoke rose from heating stones, and cooking pots with fires for butchering chickens and singeing the hair from many pigs. All was in readiness for the great feast. It was a busy, shouting, cheerful place. It was easy to see that the workmen were glad to finally be rewarded with this feast and its meaning for them for their long years of work. Bob put the finishing touches on the tractor and scraper and as he parked them, and looked it all over, he too was filled with relief and gratitude. The hours passed and the long day finally ended with Cowboy's call to gather. It was time to eat and party. Hundreds of local people found spots to sit together. Bob looked forward to the delicious food he had long ago grown to love. Uncovering the greenery-lined pits, and tossing the hot stones aside, the deliciously steamed meat was exposed. With its drippings over the vegetables and nutritious greens cooked below, the well-done meat was removed and laid out for all to witness on long rows of fresh pandanas leaves. They served Bob huge quantities of the status pig meat and heaped beef too with all its goodness in front of him. His personal pandanas leaf plate was full and did he enjoy it! While he was sitting cross legged on the ground eating with his fingers, he loudly sucked the bones with the other men. He would then wipe his greasy hands along his bared legs just as they all did. He feasted.

Cowboy then shared what he had bought with Bob's contribution. He told everyone that he had wanted to buy a cow with Bob's money and some distance away had found a man with one for sale. It seemed this one had fallen into a now dry toilet pit and broken a leg, so it was for sale. A bargain! And would be delicious. Besides, status meat was not usually available.

As the meal wound down and tummies were filled, it was now time for speeches. A very important part of it all. PNG men are people of talk, and speechmaking poured out of them naturally and with gifted oratory. Now, in the staging area, one after another, they took their stand loudly stating gratitude for Bob's work. Of course, they spoke boldly also of what they themselves and their families had done. They thanked the government for funding this project in this remote, local area, and the Church of the Nazarene for taking care of the funds and thus seeing that it got finished. They lifted up again the now achieved promise of more complete health care. Soon a long-awaited school would come with this better travel access for teachers. The coffee crop would leave directly from there and head to sale points more efficiently. Thus, the speeches went on and on so each one could have his important say.

Then it was Bob's time to talk. He too wanted to praise each and every man and especially Cowboy and Wesley, who had made his work possible. He reminded them that this was a work for God and the strip would be best used by them if they honored God with it. They were not to bring in beer and use it to hurt their community but to bless others by using it for good things for all. He reminded them he was not paid by the government nor the church to do his part but was glad to freely give his time to God. They too had worked all this time with only the hope that they might be paid one day. This was not assured but with Bob's sharing it made them feel a bit better. Perhaps they too might claim their work as a gift to God and their community. Bob encouraged them to keep the strip maintained until the government actually approved it for planes to land. That might take a while as these things usually did. They would need to keep the grass trimmed and repair any small rain drainage rills before it could cause extensive damage to the soil. They nodded in agreement and murmured among themselves. As Bob sat down, they cheered on and on.

Cowboy then told Bob it was time for him to come forward and receive gifts. News to Bob! As he rose, he saw a long line already forming with men carrying gifts for him, and he was humbled. Standing there, now being honored this way, he was amazed. One after another they came. Many bore colorful handwoven string bags, *bilums*, and hung them around his neck and heaped them on the ground at his feet. More than twenty men carried to him status gifts of handmade spears with their hardened tips and carvings along the bamboo shafts. A few pressed a coin into his hands. Cowboy wrote a note in English and folded it around a goodly sum of money with praise and blessings for Bob's work and love of God.

Finally, the long line came to an end and Bob, with bowed head, breathed a humble sigh of thanks. As he looked up again, he saw one old man slowly still coming toward him with his hand clenched around something and stretched out. His wrinkled face as well as his hobbled walk bespoke his age, yet here he was also eager to give and happy to see Bob in front of him. As Bob reached out to embrace this last one in line, the elder opened his dry and dirty hand to show on his level palm three tiny potatoes lying there. A wonder! A true gift! This new crop was being introduced into this area and here a small start was offered in gratitude. It moved Bob. He was so humbled by this. The past two years melted into this moment. As he accepted them into his own hands, he felt this as a miraculous product of what it means to be grateful. He hugged this old man and felt it was truly the greatest gift of all that day. Just three small potatoes. Just that. Just what the man had. Just what he could give. Just right. Just what it took to hit the spot with Bob. It is a memory that has never faded. It is an example that keeps on blessing him. Yes, just three tiny potatoes. Yet, it was just enough.

Chapter 14

THE PHARISEE

Well, I have to say I was warned. Before moving from our small South Dakota town to Olathe, Kansas, I was told by some community and church friends that, although the area had many Nazarene churches, it was the city and they would all be big. That would be suspect against what I had been taught and we would probably need to search for a small church where we could "really worship". It just could not be done in those "big churches". What did I know, as *I* had never worshipped in a really large church? What worldliness I would find in those big churches would probably shock and maybe sully me, was the protective advice.

My upbringing in the Midwest states of Wisconsin, Iowa, and most recently, South Dakota, was conservative, loving, and Christian. My parents agreed with the community values expressed by the general population. Ladies did not wear shorts to town. They did not wear bright red lipstick to town. They did not go to town with bare legs. They did not wear gaudy jewelry or revealing clothing. Movies were very selectively shunned by most community parents, as was the dance. Most of the area churches also felt these physical displays were signs of an uncommitted heart and often shared this with pulpit preaching. I had a large group of friends in my school and church with this same thinking, so I did not feel left out or different in any way.

My Christian life was important to me. I had been saved as a nine-year-old, kneeling in repentance at the altar of our church in Wisconsin, and began to listen to God's speaking and learning to obey Him. My parents had tried to teach me right from wrong, but I had been willful and disobedient. In church that day, when I was touched by the Holy Spirit and made to see that this same behavior hurt Jesus, not just my parents, I felt shame and conviction. From then on, I only wanted to please Him and follow closely. I loved to read my Bible and memorized many verses. Times of willfulness came up and I learned the way to keep connected to God was by always keeping a clean slate, so to speak, not letting sin keep me down. I grew in the Lord by listening to His guidance.

Part of this was in following the recommendations for a godly life set out for me by others. Much of this was external and visible. I was proud that I did not do these forbidden things, nor want to. I quickly learned to judge others spiritual status just by looking at them closely. My eyes were becoming skilled in this.

Once, as a kindergartener, a school friend painted one of my fingernails a bright red. I loved it and came home to show my Mother. She told me to "Get that off right now!" I was learning. When I was a teen, a certain gal returned home and to church after completing her secretarial schooling. She had put a bit of color on her lips and we all noted this with alarm. We ourselves did not do this! Not us! Another time, I noted a woman who seemed to enjoy worship but there were those small round earrings in her ear lobes! I learned that one could easily sense if a person was really a Christian just by looking, even from a long way off. We girls were proud that on Sunday afternoons we kept our dresses on and did not change into worldly slacks, which showed we kept the Sabbath holy. As a young mother, I would not run the vacuum on Sunday. I got on my hands and knees and, with careful fingers, picked up any food from under the high chair at the table where our kiddies had eaten. Vacuuming would have been Sabbath work!

From just looking at externals, my judgment now grew to rigid bits and pieces of "Godly Pride" expressed in "I do this! I did not do that!" I did not see it, but I was becoming an active, eager Pharisee. It was sweeping into my vision and my deeds and certainly into my heart. What I was doing had become so automatic for me it did not cross my mind that I might be headed down a sinful path.

God had plans for me though. He loved me as I was but too much to leave me that way! Now we were in Olathe because Bob had clearly felt a call from God to move from our small Dakota town and settle here in the city. Everything had miraculously fallen into place in this move. The quickly rented home, the job the next day for Bob, the settling in of our family. Our fears, given to us by others, did not materialize. No one stole our little ones off the streets. Our teen boys didn't get into drugs or alcohol, and now we were trying out the churches. After the warnings we were wary. Still, we had decided to go to the "Big One" for just their grand opening services. We would then keep looking for that small one where we could "really worship."

College Church's beautiful new construction, steeple, and stained-glass window drew us. It was on the edge of the campus of the new Mid-America Nazarene College (now University), not far from our home. That first Sunday settled it for us. There was great preaching, Holy Spirit moving, and people finding God at the altar in both Sunday morning and evening services. Later we looked at each other and asked, *"Didn't we sense the Holy Spirit here? Didn't we see God moving? Didn't we really worship?"* We did not need to keep looking for a church. We knew God had led us to this very one, one at which we would experience no compromise, either.

People here were different though. Many were moving in from distant parts of the country just as we had. The city was booming and the church and college were experiencing this also. We found we loved the change and stimulation of differentness in the way we now lived as city folk.

My mind loved this early adjustment, but my Pharisee's heart and eyes were still active.

One Sunday, as I walked down the long corridor in back of the sanctuary, it seemed to me that it was totally empty except for me and a woman of the church who was walking toward me from the distance. Shockingly, I instantly saw that here was what I had been warned about. Right in front of my eyes! Here she came. I could see that her blond hair was probably not natural. Were those thin eyebrows plucked? Tiny twinkles were barely visible at her ears, but I noted them! Was that an extra ring on her finger? Then, there were those lips with lipstick on them! Yes, here it was. Here in this big church. I could see it now! I had been warned!

As she neared my Pharisaical heart she brightened with a smile and began to greet me cheerfully. "Well, I''s so good to see you, Bessie! We are so glad you and your family have moved here and sense a blessing from you. Our church just loves to welcome you and the many others to our services and to what God is doing here. He has done so many miracles in us all and we see your coming too as a blessing. You will add to our church and God is leading us all. We want to do what He wants us to do together." She spoke on and on with cheer and love and greeting in Christ's name. As she did, I saw her genuine Christlikeness revealed in attitude and heart and voice.

Suddenly, I saw myself, a modern, biblical Pharisee! I was a judge! I was the one with the "cup all clean on the outside, but dirty and unwashed on the inside." My heart melted with conviction as I saw this and I repented in spirit right there and then. God literally washed over my whole body and soul and mind at that moment. I was changed! I would never be the same again. My heart was washed. So were my eyes. I experienced healing!

We remained in that church and, six years later, I saw some of God's special purpose in this healing of my Pharisaical heart and eyes. God called us to be missionaries. Our first assignment, among Native Americans, was to a culture where almost everyone was covered with jewelry! Beautifully hand-crafted silver and turquoise adorned tiny babies, women, and even men. It was a form of banking, I learned. In love, they even covered me with it! I became immune to it all. My eyes just never saw it!

Our second assignment some years later, was to the Latin world where lovely clothes and attention to body was important. Attire was more important than food for many, and some could even tailor perfectly fitted suits and wedding gowns. Necklines and faces received attention as did cosmetics. With my new heart's vision, I never saw these details...only loveliness and loving spirits.

The next two decades were spent in the South Pacific where a lot of clothing was optional, and skin was apparent. Often, in the tropics, very little was worn yet their modesty was carefully apparent. A man might sit in church wearing a t-shirt and with a bunch of leaves at his backside listening in worship there. A mother could publicly nurse her baby. Toddler boys needn't wear anything at all. All this skin just covered wonderful people whom God loved. A loving God showed me this with my new heart and eyes.

I am amazed at how God prepares us for what he has in store for us. They say that God doesn't call the prepared; He prepares the called—or different versions of that. Knowing what was in store for Bob and me, the work in foreign countries and different cultures, all my life experiences were in fact preparation for our missions assignments. Hindsight is a wonderful lens to see this through, even if I didn't see it at the time.

God knew what I needed to become to serve Him, so He changed me. He gave me a new set of eyes and a new heart. He took the now-changed Pharisee and put her where He planned for her to serve. Thanks be to God, I never again returned to judgment on externals. That had really taken a lot of energy that I needed to use to be what He wanted me to be...accepting, loving. Christian. I am forever and eternally grateful.

Made in the USA
Columbia, SC
08 June 2019